PROFESSIONAL
SIGNIFICATORS

in Traditional Astrology

Öner Döşer, AMA, ISAR CAP

Edited with a Preface by
BENJAMIN N. DYKES, PhD

The Cazimi Press
Minneapolis, Minnesota
2018

Published and printed in the United States of America

First American edition published by:
The Cazimi Press
Minneapolis, MN

Translation by:
Sibel Oltulu

Edited by:
Mustafa Konur, Sibel Oltulu, and Benjamin N. Dykes

Original design by:
Mustafa Konur
mustafakonur@gmail.com

AstroArt Astroloji ve Danışmanlık Ltd. Şti.
Bağdat Cad. No. 284 Canoğlu Apt.
Kat: 3 Daire: 20 Kadıköy/İstanbul
Tel: 0216 386 73 96
www.astrolojiokulu.com
info@astrolojiokulu.com
Certificate No: 22202

ISBN-13: 978-1-934586-47-1

TABLE OF CONTENTS

PREFACE

This book is part of a new series in support of the traditional astrology courses of the AstroArt Astrology School in Istanbul, headed by my friend and colleague Öner Döşer. It follows our successful 2015 release of his popular *Astrological Prediction: A Handbook of Techniques* (2015).

After a long career in Istanbul's oldest and most prestigious bazaar, Öner followed his heart and turned fully to astrology, soon becoming one of the leading astrologers in Turkey, with numerous television appearances and books to his credit. His Astrology School Publishing has released 14 well-received books, not to mention his own articles in international astrological publications. Since 2012 he has been the organizer of the highly successful International Astrology Days in Istanbul.

Öner Döşer's blends traditional and modern techniques and attitudes. For example, for the most part he uses Placidus houses, but for certain techniques he focuses on whole signs. In terms of planets, he uses the three outers as well as Chiron. However, he grounds his work in traditional authors, such as Ptolemy, Dorotheus, Firmicus Maternus, Māshā'allāh, Sahl, Abū Ma'shar, Schoener, Lilly, and others. For this new series I have largely provided my own translations of the source material (both current and forthcoming), with sentence numbers in boldface in the footnotes. In some cases, I have updated older translations to reflect my current thinking. I have also added a few comments of my own, prefaced with **BD**.

I know you will enjoy these succinct and helpful guides to astrological interpretation, and your chart reading will improve as a result.

Benjamin Dykes, 2018

INTRODUCTION

The significators in a natal chart do not only signify the native's personal characteristics and psychological profile. Within a chart there are many significators which signify the native's health, money, profession, children, other people in his life, and many other things. These crucial significators may be determined through certain special techniques, and help us make more precise and detailed predictions regarding the native's life.

The issues that attract the attention of contemporary astrologers seem to differ from those of the ancient astrologers. The greatest difference between traditional and contemporary astrology is that traditionally the planets in a chart are not only attributed to the native, but also to other people signified through these planets. Traditional astrology is based on distinguishing and determining the planets which signify different issues.

First of all, we need to consider what a significator represents by its nature. According to traditional astrologers, the Sun represents the native's father in particular, but also all male figures who are authoritative in the native's life. The Moon signifies the native's mother in particular, but is also the general significator of female figures. She is also considered when determining the native's health problems. Mercury is related generally to all siblings, whereas Mars is related to brothers especially. The native's mind is busy in the matters of the house where Mercury is located, and this house indicates where we use our talents. We are faced with challenges, hatred, and aggression in the house where Mars is located. Venus represents young women, wives, and also young sisters. We find joy and pleasure where Venus is located in the chart. Jupiter and Saturn represent wisdom. Jupiter is also related to wealthy people, financial wealth, where ease and freedom is, and also genuine feelings and sincerity. In nocturnal charts Saturn represents the father and grandfathers, poor people, and hard work. There is fear where Saturn is located in the chart.

These significators are interpreted through the houses they are located in, as well as their zodiacal positions, to delineate the people and issues they are attributed to. For example, the location of Venus, the houses she rules, and her aspects, give us information about the people and events delineated by this planet. Let's assume Venus is in the 12th house: we may interpret that the native's sister is his secret enemy. Let's assume Venus is also burned and squares Saturn: so, this sister may be ill or fighting against difficulties.

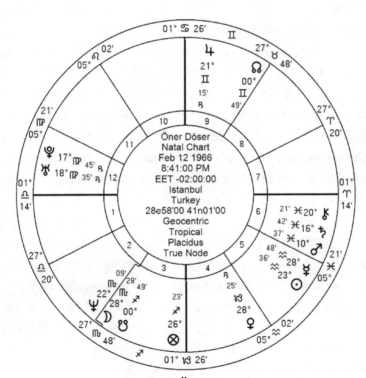

Figure 1: Öner Döşer

Let's think of a chart with Venus in the 4th house. As Venus is physically placed here, she is the accidental significator of the 4th house.

So, she shapes the issues of the 4th house according to her own nature, which helps us predict events related to the 4th. In addition, Venus brings her Venusian nature to bear on the 4th, by means of the houses she rules. Let's assume Venus is the domicile lord of the 1st, 2nd, and 9th houses, and the exaltation lord of the 6th. As she is located in the 4th, she links the issues of these houses to the 4th.

If there is more than one planet in a house, each planet shows its impact in its own time, starting with the planet which is closest to the house cusp. For example, let's assume that Mars, the Sun, and Mercury are in the 11th house, and Mars is the closest one to the house cusp. If the other planets in this house (the Sun and Mercury), do not rule this house (that is, if they are not the domicile or exaltation lords, or the victor), then Mars will dominate the events related to this house. This means Mars is the accidental significator of the matters related to the 11th house. The native's friends, social environment, income earned from his profession, his hopes and expectations, are all ruled by Mars. The issues related to the other houses ruled by Mars will automatically be linked to the issues of the 11th. Let's remember our golden rule: being physically present in a house is superior to what a planet signifies by its rulership of other houses.

In the example chart below (Figure 2) which belongs to my dear teacher Robert Zoller, since Mars is both physically present in this house and one of the lords of this house (as exaltation lord and victor), and also the nearest planet to the house cusp, he is the accidental significator of issues related to the 11th house. It means that the people and events represented by the 11th are of a Martial nature: disagreeable, conflicting, competitive, aggressive, irritated, ambitious, leaders, brave, direct, unreliable, etc. If Venus were the significator of the 11th house, then the native's friends would be Venusian types: pretty, moderate, compatible, elegant, cheerful, and playful.

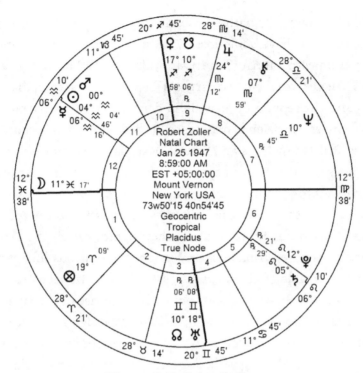

Figure 2: Robert Zoller

When making a judgment, we should also consider the aspects of the significator in addition to its house location and rulerships. In our example Mars, the significator of the 11th house, is in conjunction with the Sun and Mercury, and in opposition with Saturn. We may judge that the native has competitive and conflicting relations with his friends. There may be a leadership struggle among them. The native's friends are Martian types. As Mars is in Aquarius and rules the 9th house, his friends may have radical ideas and original ideologies. They may also be interested in the sciences and astrology as well. As Mars rules the 9th house of this chart, the native's friends may be foreigners, people from academia, or involved in other 9th house issues, or his friends may encourage him in investments because Mars is the lord of the 2nd house and the Lot of Fortune. Perhaps the native will earn money through some organi-

zation or group. The native's friends may be involved in secret affairs, or ill, or have some losses, because Mars is burned and in
opposition with Saturn (Saturn also rules the 12ᵗʰ house). The native's friends may be his partners because Mars conjoins with
Mercury. His reputation may be in danger due to his friends and
social circles. His friends may cause his bad reputation because the
Sun is afflicted by Mars and Saturn: Mars as the significator of the
11ᵗʰ house, and Saturn as the domicile lord of the 11ᵗʰ, represent
the native's friends and social groups.

Moreover, there are other significators specific to a topic. Although they differ in each chart, they signify certain issues like
marriage, children, finances, profession, the religious life, etc. By
preparing a table of victors as suggested by traditional astrologers
(see Appendix B), we may determine the dignities of the significators. The zodiacal state of the significator (the sign and house it is
in, its aspects, the state of its lord) help us determine the course of
the topic we are dealing with. For example, for the issues related to
marriage we need to find the Marriage Victor. So, we need the zodiacal degrees of the significators related to marriage, which are:

1. The cusp of the 7ᵗʰ house.
2. The lord of the 7ᵗʰ house.
3. Venus.
4. The Lot of marriage and its lord.
5. The first triplicity lord of the 7ᵗʰ house.

If the victor over these significators are harmoniously configured with the lord of the Ascendant, then the native has a
harmonious marriage—whereas their incompatibility indicates a
negative course of marriage. If these significators (or the strongest
one of them) is in angular or succeedent houses, if they are not in
contact with the malefics, not burned, retrograde, or in cadent
houses, and if they are in contact with the lord of the Ascendant,

then the marriage will be a good and proper one. (See Appendix B for how to calculate a victor.)

The purpose of this book

In this book I will describe how traditional astrologers determined the professional significator and how they used all of the significators in judgments, providing some examples so that astrology students may easily understand these techniques. My primary purpose is to introduce these methodical and reliable techniques to contemporary astrologers.

My own specialty is in the medieval period of the Art of astrology, but through other references (in addition to those from my dear teacher and master Robert Zoller), I also aim to introduce you to the rules and techniques used by the ancient astrologers. In addition to this book on professional significators, you may also want to explore my books on other important significators. I believe that astrology students who modestly and diligently practice these methods and rules of the older masters, will easily determine the significators in a chart and make correct interpretations.

I hope this book reminds students of astrology that the traditional techniques are methodical and efficient, and help restore the inextricable link between today's astrology and its traditional origins.

Öner Döşer
Astroart School of Astrology, ASA, Istanbul, Turkey
http://www.astrolojiokulu.com/en

1: PROFESSIONAL SIGNIFICATORS

The oldest information we have on this subject is based on Claudius Ptolemy's works. Although many contributions were made later on, Ptolemy's methods have always been important. Unlike contemporary astrologers, ancient astrologers began with the Ascendant when determining the professional significator. Bonatti suggests we should see if there is any planet in the 1st house: if now, only then may we see if there are any planets in the 10th house.[1] Today, we first look at the Midheaven (MC), the sign on the MC, the lord of this sign, and then the planets which aspect the MC. Often, the difference between modern and traditional approaches is that the issues which are analyzed first in modern astrology, are analyzed later in traditional methods. Although this difference may seem to be trivial, it is really crucial, because a mistake in the order of methods may cause incorrect delineations.

In the example chart below which belongs to an engineer (Figure 3), you see Scorpio is on the MC. We cannot relate Scorpio to civil engineering directly. Mars, the lord of the MC, is in the 8th house of the chart, and in Libra. This does not indicate engineering, either. However, the native is an engineer. When we have a look at the planets in the 1st house and close to the Ascendant, we see Saturn in Capricorn and Jupiter nearby. Saturn is related to engineering and Jupiter is related to finances in general. The native is a high level finance executive, signified by Jupiter in the 1st house (and also by the Sun in the 8th), in a privately-held company where he has been working for many years.

---

[1] Bonatti, Tr. IX.3, 10th House, Ch. 1 (p. 1,337).

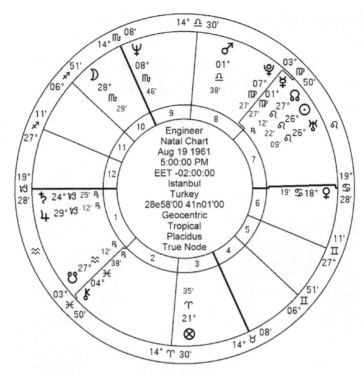

Figure 3: Engineer

Traditionally, the Sun is also considered a crucial starting point, even as a kind of Ascendant. However, we are not referring to the Sun sign (as in modern astrology). Here we should look at the eastern planet(s) or the planets aspecting the Sun, to find the significator of the profession. The same is true for the Moon. According to traditional views, the professional significator is the planet which rises before the Sun (eastern), or the planet which rises after the Moon (western), especially if that planet is located in one of the angular houses (the 1st, 10th, 7th, and 4th). But at this point, we need to clarify an issue. Superior planets (planets beyond the Sun) are stronger when they are astronomically eastern of (i.e. rising before) the Sun, while inferior planets (the Moon, Mercury, Venus) are stronger when they are astronomically western of (i.e., rising after) the Sun. But since being "eastern" is emphasized in ancient texts, Robert Zoller, the contemporary master of medieval astrology, put it that Mercury and Venus should be treated as *astrologically* "eastern" and strong when they rise after the Sun. I would like to clarify this with my own chart as an example.

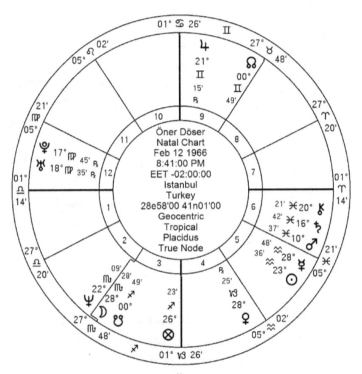

Figure 4: Öner Döşer

Here, Venus is the only planet located in an angular house. Since she rises before the Sun, we may identify her as being astronomically eastern; however, according to Zoller she is astrologically "western" when in this position, and so is less strong. On the other hand, Mercury (who rises after the Sun) is astronomically western but it is again astrologically "eastern" (and so *is* strong). But both Venus and Mercury are western of the *Moon*, and both make aspects with her. Since the Moon's rulership of the MC automatically makes her a candidate for being the professional significator, the westernness of Mercury and Venus from her and their aspects to her make them possible candidates, too, apart from their relation to the Sun.

But let's assume there are two or more planets in angular houses, both of them eastern of the Sun (or even western of the Moon, although that is secondary in importance). Which of them should we choose? We should choose the one which is in the stronger position. All planets located in angular houses may be a significator for the profession if they are eastern of the Sun (or western of the Moon), because they represent the native's strongest talents. If several planets fulfill these criteria, the order of choice depends on the order of strength suggested by the traditional astrologers: the 1st, 10th, 7th, and 4th. For example, if one of these planets is in the 1st house and the other in the 10th, we prefer the one in the 1st; if one is in the 10th and the other in the 7th, we prefer the 10th.

Let's have a look at the example chart below (Figure 5). Here Venus, Jupiter, and Saturn are located in angular houses. Being angular, each of them may be a significator of the profession. Venus in the 1st has priority over both Jupiter in the 7th and Saturn in the 4th. Venus is the strongest among them and also the only one which aspects the MC, which is a very important factor in determining the significator. So, we can prefer Venus to the other two significators. The chart belongs to Sertap Erener,[2] a very famous singer (a profession related to Venus in general). Venus is also in conjunction with Alphecca and Acrux in this chart, and these fixed stars increase the impact of Venus.

---

[2] https://en.wikipedia.org/wiki/Sertab_Erener.

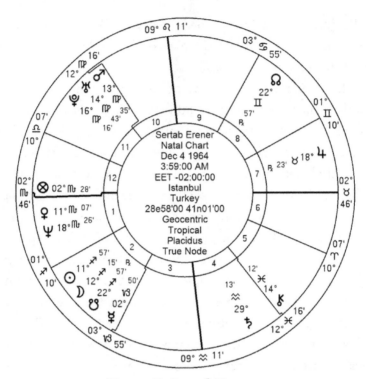

Figure 5: Sertab Erener

If both planets which are possible professional significators are in the same house, then prefer the one which is more favorably placed in the zodiac (more dignified, less afflicted by malefics, direct, and aspecting its lord) or which is closer to the house cusp. I personally prefer the one closer to the house cusp.

As an example, let's look at the chart below (Figure 6): Here there are two planets in the 10th house, and Mercury is closer to the cusp. Venus is peregrine while Mercury is in detriment. Even though the native is busy with Mercurial things (he is engaged in trade), he sells souvenirs and ornaments: this means that both Venus and Mercury contribute to the native's profession, but Mercury's contribution is more fundamental, because he is closer to the cusp.

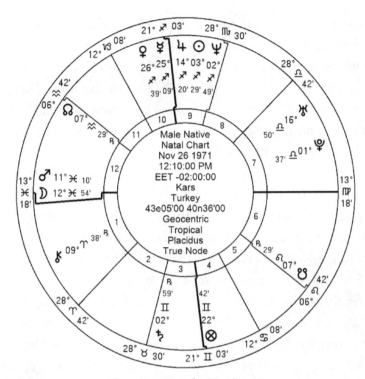

Figure 6: Male Native 1

Ancient astrologers who used Ptolemy's methods especially considered two factors for determining the professional significator: the Sun and the sign on the MC.[3] A planet which is eastern of the Sun may be the professional significator (especially if it is aspected by the Moon), whether or not it is located at the MC, but a planet which is both eastern of the Sun and at the MC is undoubtedly the only professional significator. If however there are two planets, one of which is eastern of the Sun and the other in the MC and aspected by the Moon, then two of them may be considered as the significator: the one which is more strongly placed and dignified should be preferred. If none of the planets fits these circumstances, then the lord of the MC should be the professional significator.[4]

---

[3] *Tet.*IV.4 (Robbins p. 381).
[4] *Tet.* IV.4 (Robbins pp. 381-83.

Schoener, who made use of Ptolemy's studies and sometimes made some additions to them, notes: "...but give priority to the one which is victorious according to the multitude of testimonies in the place of the Sun, to the Midheaven or the Ascendant,[5] and you will determine the native's office by means of each."[6] I interpret this to mean that we should look for the planet which is more dignified amongst the possible significators.

If we look at the example chart above, we see that Jupiter has the most testimonies, based on his rulership of the Ascendant (Pisces), the MC (Sagittarius), and the Sun (Sagittarius). Although he is burned, he is the most powerful candidate for being the professional significator because he is the lord of the MC, in contact with the Sun and Moon, in his own domicile and triplicity. Although he is western of the Sun and eastern of the Moon, he is direct, fast, and also in his *hayyiz*, a sect-related condition.[7] The native deals with international trade businesses, as Mercury is conjoined with the MC, and the lord of both Mercury and the MC (i.e., Jupiter) is in the 9th.

---

[5] **BD**: As a description of Ptolemy's method, Schoener has gotten things wrong, in part because Ptolemy does not mention the Ascendant. But Ptolemy *does* seem to think that we ought to favor the victor over the place of the candidate planet (or maybe the Sun) as well as the Midheaven. So Schoener is right to look for a victor, and may have done some creative interpretation by following others in adding the Ascendant. The question is whether the printed edition of Schoener is accurate and we really should prefer the victor over the place of the Sun to the others, or—as Döşer sees it here—Schoener really wants the victor over the three places mentioned here. Later (**59**), Schoener reports the views of "others" as: "The significator of the mastery is the one which was found in the Ascendant or Midheaven, eastern of the Sun and western of the Moon."

[6] Schoener, I.11, **4**.

[7] **BD**: That is, he is a diurnal planet above the earth in a diurnal chart, and also in a sign of his own gender (male).

Based on knowledge transmitted by the ancient astrologers, Johannes Schoener summarizes the points which should be used for determining the native's profession:[8]

1. The 10th house.
2. The lord of the 10th house.
3. Venus, Mercury, and Mars.
4. Victor of the possible significators for profession.
5. The Lot of profession.[9]
6. The first triplicity lord of the 10th house.

The Victor

Bonatti suggests that when there are no planets in the four angular houses, we should find the victors[10] of these houses:[11] that is, we need to find the planets which have the highest dignities in the signs located on the cusps of the 1st, 10th, 7th, and 4th houses. These four victors are all possible significators of the profession. To clarify, please see the example chart below:[12]

---

[8] Schoener, I.11, **49-58**.
[9] **BD**: Schoener: "The Lot of work and mastery." Schoener does not seem to define this Lot. But see Döşer's preferred version below.
[10] **BD**: This is often transliterated from Arabic as *almuten* or *al-mubtazz*.
[11] Bonatti Tr. IX.3, 10th House, Ch. 1 (p. 1,338).
[12] See also Appendices B and C.

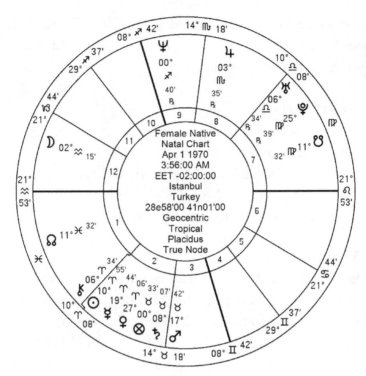

Figure 7: Female Native

In this chart no planets are in the angular houses except the impersonal planets and Chiron. So, as suggested by Bonatti, we need to determine the victor of the angular houses. While making the calculation for discovering the victor, we assign 5 points to the domicile lord, 4 points for the exalted lord (if any), 3 points for each triplicity lord, 2 points for the bound lord, and 1 point for the face lord. In this chart the victors of the four angular houses are:

Victor of the 1st house: Saturn.
Victor of the 10th house: Jupiter.
Victor of the 7th house: Sun.
Victor of the 4th house: Mercury.

Secondly, we need to determine the victor over all of these victors, due to its rulership over their degrees:

Saturn at 8° Taurus
Jupiter at 3° Scorpio
Sun at 10° Aries
Mercury at 19° Aries

We find that Mars is the victor over all of these degrees.[13] After
determining that he is a possible significator of the profession, we
should also see how he is located in the chart. In this chart, Mars
seems to be a less powerful significator.

'Umar al-Tabarī, who says we should consider the MC and its
lord, the Sun, the Lot of work and its lord to determine the professional significator, suggests we find the victor of the profession
from all of them.[14] According to 'Umar, the victor over all these
significators, its nature and its aspect with the victor over the Ascendant, are important. Planets which make aspects with the
victor are also important in determining the quality of the profession, as well as the combination of the professional victor and the
victor over the Ascendant. He says: "If [the victor of the profes-
sion] were Mercury, the native will be a scribe and astrologer and
mathematician; and if it were the Sun, the native will be a prince
or king, and he will be very wise in the ordering of the kingdom,
and of good discretion. You will speak likewise from the nature of
this victor and of those looking at it, whether [the victor] was one
or many; and even look at the victor, and see which of the planets

---

[13] **BD**: Because three of these points are in signs ruled by Mars, we can al-
ready see that he is likely to be the victor even before making any
calculation.
[14] Al-Tabarī, *TBN* III.9 (p. 68). **BD**: That is, the victor over all of the professional significators just mentioned.

is looking at it, and mingle their work with every work of the victor. And speak according to this."[15]

By the way, let me inform you about the Lot of profession.[16] Here are two different formulas (I prefer and use the former one):

Ascendant + Moon – Saturn (by day and night), from Bonatti.[17]
Ascendant + MC - Sun (by day and night), from Valens.[18]

Schoener also notes that the victor of the possible significators for profession should be determined. The degrees to be considered are:[19]

1. The cusp of the 10th house.
2. The lord of the 10th house.
3. The Sun.
4. The Lot of profession.[20]
5. The first triplicity lord of the 10th house.

The planet which is the victor over all of these degrees is the victor of the profession. The nature of this planet, its zodiacal state, its determination by house or place, and its aspects, are crucial in determining the profession (or the professional talents) of the native. (Zodiacal state is determined by the essential dignities and debilities. Planetary aspects also have a bearing on the zodiacal state.)[21]

---

[15] Al-Tabarī, *TBN* III.9 (pp. 69-70).
[16] **BD**: There are many names for this kind of Lot, and many different calculations. Döşer is using the general term "Lot of profession."
[17] Bonatti, Tr. VIII.2, Ch. 13, p. 1,077. (See also *ITA* VI.2.40.)
[18] See al-Qabīsī in *ITA* VI.2.42.
[19] Schoener I.11, **74-80**.
[20] **BD**: Schoener: "The Lot of work."
[21] Zoller, *Foundation* Lesson 1, p. 37; *Diploma* Lesson 6, p. 38.

The Difference between Diurnal and Nocturnal Charts

Another difference between traditional and modern astrology is the distinction between diurnal and nocturnal (that is, day and night) charts. Traditional astrologers would note whether the chart was diurnal or nocturnal.

If a native is born by day and the Moon was waxing, then we would look at the New and Full Moon prior to the birth and see with whom the Moon would first connect after leaving the Sun (or if a nocturnal chart, see the planet which first joins with the Lot of Fortune). So, this planet would be considered the professional significator no matter what the nature of that aspect is. To summarize, a chart where the Sun is over the horizon (in the 12th, 11th, 10th, 9th, 8th, or 7th houses) is a diurnal chart, while a chart with the Sun under the horizon (in the 1st, 2nd, 3rd, 4th, 5th, or 6th houses) is a nocturnal one. To determine the professional significator, like all other significators, it is crucial to know if the chart is diurnal or nocturnal. In a diurnal chart, the planet which the Moon first aspects after leaving the prenatal New or Full Moon is considered to be one of the possible significators for the profession. If we have a nocturnal chart, then we should consider the planet which will make the first aspect with the Lot of Fortune.[22]

Please see the example chart below (Figure 8). It is a diurnal chart and the pre-natal New Moon occurred at 25° Taurus. This pre-natal New Moon makes a trine with Jupiter at 26° Virgo. So, Jupiter is one of the possible professional significators.

---

[22] Bonatti, Tr. IX.3, 10th House, Ch. 1, p. 1,338.

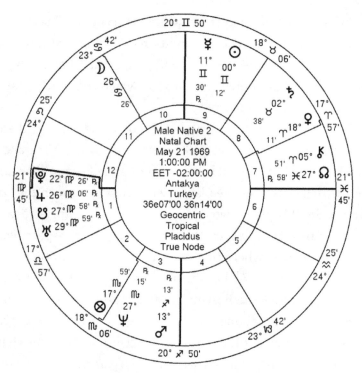

Figure 8: Male Native 2

Let's also give an example for nocturnal charts. Below (Figure 9) you may see my chart, which is nocturnal. The Sun is the first planet to aspect the Lot of Fortune, and he is one of its triplicity lords (the Lot is in a fiery sign, Sagittarius). So, the Sun is a possible professional significator.[23]

---

[23] Bonatti says that in a nocturnal chart we should prefer the planet which the Moon connects with, or she most recently separated from, or the lord of the house in which the Lot of Fortune is, or the planet better disposed (Tr. IX.3, 10th House, Ch. 1, p. 1,339).

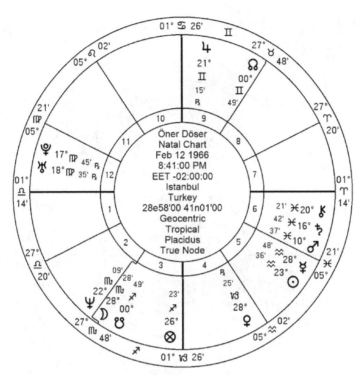

Figure 9: Öner Döşer

Unlike other traditional authors, Bonatti suggests another point: look at any planet "newly appearing from under the rays of the Sun, removed from him not by more than 20° (if it were one of the superiors, let it be eastern from him, if however it were of the inferiors, let it be western)."[24] Let's practice on the example chart below. Jupiter in the 10th house of the chart is 18° away from the Sun, and is eastern. Venus in the 11th house is 18° away from the Sun and is astrologically eastern. So, these two possible significators of the profession are separating from the rays and getting stronger, but their distance has not exceeded 20°. As a result, both of them may be considered as professional significators. Due to his

---

[24] Bonatti, Tr. IX.3, 10th House, Ch. 1, p. 1,338.

better zodiacal position, and as he is the lord of the MC, Jupiter should be preferred.

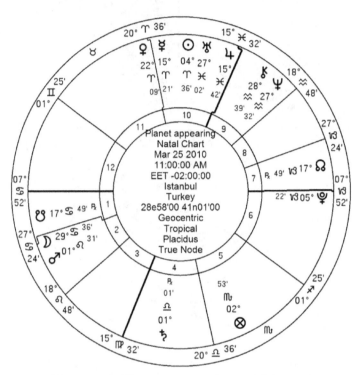

Figure 10: Planet appearing within 20°

Universal significators of profession

As noted in other traditional texts, three planets are called "universal" significators of the profession: Mercury, Venus, and Mars. According to the ancient astrologers, these three planets should be made specific to the profession according to the signs and houses they are in. So, what gives these three priority?

The ancients considered the Sun and the Moon as being too supreme and lofty to be professional significators. As noted by Zoller, the Sun (the creator of life) was considered the King, while the Moon (the creator of the body) was considered the Queen: and a King and Queen do not have trade professions. So, the luminaries were not suitable for being professional significators. Then, as Jupiter represents the priesthood and as this was not exactly a trade profession but a hereditary calling, Jupiter was not considered a professional significator. Saturn, representing farmers and farms (and as farming was something one was born to), was not taken as a professional significator. So, one is left with Mars, Venus, and Mercury as professional significators.[25]

As the professions were not that varied and specialized in ancient times, Mars represented warriors and those involved in works requiring brute force; Venus represented artisans in general, and Mercury the merchants and scribes. Each of these universal significators is considered as a second Ascendant, and planets aspecting each may be important as modifying the profession.[26] We will get into the details in the coming chapter.

According to Bonatti, when no planets meet these above-mentioned conditions, the planet in contact with the Sun in a diurnal chart should be preferred as the professional significator, while the planet in contact with the Moon in a nocturnal chart should be preferred. However, if the Moon is not applying to a planet, then the planet from which the Moon has separated should be taken, or the lord of the Lot of Fortune—and between the two of them, the one which is in its dignity should be preferred as the primary significator of the profession.[27]

According to Abū 'Alī, if none of the universal significators of profession (Mercury, Venus, and Mars) are in angular houses, then the lord of the 10th house should be considered in a diurnal chart, while the planet to which the Moon next applies after birth is considered in a nocturnal chart, especially if this planet has a dignity in the sign of the Lot of Fortune.[28]

---

[25] Zoller, *Diploma* Lesson 12, p. 7.
[26] Zoller, *Diploma* Lesson 12, p. 8.
[27] Bonatti, Tr. IX.3, 10th House, Ch. 1, p. 1,339.
[28] Al-Khayyāt, *JN* Ch. 33.

According to Schoener,[29] if the universal significators cannot be the significator of the profession,[30] then the lord of the MC should be taken as the significator in a diurnal chart, while the planet that the Moon next applies to should be taken in a nocturnal chart (especially if this planet is in its dignity in the place of the Lot of Fortune). However, if the Moon is empty or void in course, then the strongest of the following should be the significator of the profession:

1. The planet from which the Moon separates.
2. The lord of the Moon's sign.
3. The lord of the Lot of Fortune.
4. The lord of the Lot's sign or bound.

Meanwhile, Schoener notes that for people born while the Moon is empty in course: "The Moon being empty in course, signifies that the native will be idle, and will love to go through the mountains and deserts."[31]

According to Schoener,[32] the planet which rises before the Sun (having gone out from his rays) or the planet which is located in the MC and connects by aspect with the Moon should be determined as the significator of the profession. But if there is no planet that rises before the Sun, then the planet located in the MC and aspecting the Moon should be the significator of the profession. If there is no planet rising before the Sun *nor* any planet located in the MC, then the victor of the MC should be the significator of the profession. When the professional significator is determined, then we should see if it makes aspects with the universal significators (Mars, Venus and Mercury): if so, then it

---

[29] Schoener I.11, **64-65**.
[30] **BD**: That is, because they are not in an angle (per Schoener).
[31] Schoener I.11, **84**.
[32] Schoener I.11, **1-7**.

becomes certain that this planet is the significator of the profession. Additionally, the planet which is the victor of the pre-natal New or Full Moon may also be taken as a significator of the profession, because the native is also active in the subjects represented by this planet.[33]

Other details on profession

The strongest of the possible professional significators signifies the native's ideal professional talent. The aspects of this planet are also important. For example, if Mercury is the professional significator, then the native deals with professions that require expression and interpretation, and he may be a journalist, author, public relations expert, teacher, or astrologer. If Mercury is most closely aspecting Jupiter, the native may perform his profession in the international arena: for example, he may be an international author, teacher, speaker, or international relations expert. As commonly agreed by traditional astrologers, the Mercury-Jupiter conjunction or aspects indicate a highly successful speaker and one who makes right and fair judgements. Lilly states:

> "Mercury in conjunction or aspect with Jupiter makes excellent orators, of great justice in judging causes, circumspect and just in rendering the law, equally moderate in refraining from anything..."[34]

When there is more than one significator of profession, or planets that aspect the significator, Ptolemy states in his famous *Tetrabiblos* that the native may use various talents. For example, if Mercury and Venus are the two significators, the native's actions will be artistic, literary, and musical, "particularly when they have

---

[33] Schoener I.11, **85**.
[34] Lilly, *CA* III.149 (p. 627).

exchanged places. For they produce workers in the theatre, actors, dealers in slaves, makers of musical instruments, members of the chorus...And again, if Saturn testifies to them, he produces those in the aforesaid callings, as well as dealers in feminine finery. If Jupiter testifies, he produces lawyers, supervisors of counting houses, public officers, teachers of children, leaders of the populace."[35]

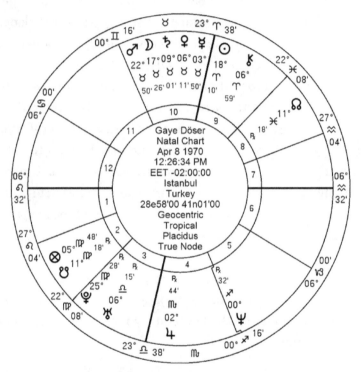

Figure 11: Gaye Döşer

Ptolemy's magnificent analysis correctly describes the profession of a woman who is living centuries after him: my wife. As you can, Mercury and Venus located in her 10th house conjoin with Saturn. My wife is an artisan who makes and sells ornaments for

---

[35] *Tet.* IV.4 (Robbins p. 387).

women. This proves that the findings of traditional astrologers are still valid. I will mention other details in the coming paragraphs based on William Lilly's findings as well.

Joined significators

Aspects to the professional significator indicate the native's attitude towards his profession, and his working style. To clarify, I would like to quote from Firmicus Maternus: "For, Mars presenting the testimony will make leaders bold, dangerous,[36] moving quickly, and who err in every way, and who are never subjugated by the will of any authority. But Saturn brings about mild people, profound, quiet, and haughty, and who <do> all things with dissimulation. And you ought to observe this for the other two stars, too—which if all of it were gathered together by you in a careful manner, you would be able to explain the entire substance of [the life's] decree in the truest way: and thus the moral qualities of men would be given shape by you, just as in the manner of a painting all outlines of bodies might be made out by you, and the hidden effect of [their] moral qualities would be discovered."[37]

The astrologers who lived between the Claudius Ptolemy and William Lilly gave information on professional talents based on planetary pairs. Let me exemplify this with a summary based on *Tet.* IV.4 (Robbins pp. 383-89):

---

[36] *Periculosos.* **BD**: This could also be understood in terms of risk-taking: in other words, their life has risks and dangers.
[37] Firmicus Maternus, *Mathesis* IV.21.

4-☿	Lawmakers, orators, sophists, having familiarity with eminent people.
4-♀	Athletes, deemed worthy of honors, men being advanced due to women.
4-♂	Soldiers, servants, publicans, innkeepers, ferrymen, assistants at sacrifices.
4-♂-♀	Frequenters of temples, augurs, supervisors of women, match-makers.
4-☿-♀	Lawyers, supervisors of counting-houses, public officers, teachers of children, leaders of the populace.

The talents and professions of Mercury when he is the significator and contacting other planets is summarized here, based on Lilly's *Christian Astrology* III (pp. 627-28):

☿-♄	Performing servile offices for other men, leading a miserable life around churches, begging or agitating the affairs of the church.
☿-♂	Farmers, sailors, shepherds, cow-keepers, curriers, butchers, tailors, stonecutters or carvers, interpreters of dreams, sorcerers, the superstitious.
☿-4	Excellent orators, of great justice in judging cases, thoughtful and just in rendering the law, moderate in refraining from things, the friends of great persons, divines, lawyers, rhetoricians, judges, bankers or money-changers.
☿-☉	If not retrograde or burned, but in the heart of the Sun or in any of his dignities: associating with magistrates and men of great fortunes, scribes, treasurers, public accountants for the state, councilors, great justices. If Mars has testimony: chemistry, clipping or stamping coins, especially if Saturn has an aspect.

☿-♀	Eloquence, a great variety of manners.
☿-☽	Increases understanding, desiring to know future things, inclined to divination, especially if the Moon applies to Mercury in Taurus, Capricorn, or Cancer; if in Virgo or Scorpio, astrologers; in Aries, Leo, or Libra, divining things to come without a trained art; in Sagittarius or Pisces, interested in magic.

The role of the signs in determining professions

In traditional texts, signs are evaluated by their elements and qualities, in terms of professions they signify. The following table summarizes categories found in Lilly:[38]

Movable	Arts requiring "wits," like geometry, medicine, astrology.
Fixed (but not ♏)	Learning or education.
Human (♊ ♍ ♎ ♒)	The liberal arts, taught by authorities.
Watery & earthy (♋ ♏ ♓ ♉ ♑)	Professions around water and the earth, fields, herbs, medicine, ships, fish, funerals.
Four-footed (♈ ♌ ♐)	Mechanical professions, butchers, builders, curriers, stone-cutters, clothiers, wool-winders.

---

[38] *CA* III.149, p. 632.

Lilly also draws on Abū Bakr, who summarizes some professions by element in the following way:[39]

Fiery	Professions using fire: blacksmiths, crafts-men, bakers, glass-makers.
Earthy	Professions using earth: potters, masons, diggers.
Airy	Singers, jesters, birdcatchers.
Watery	Fishermen, launderers, fullers.

In his book on horary questions (*CA* II), Lilly gives individual professions for each sign in which the professional significator is located:[40]

♈	Cart-maker, coach-maker, shepherd, driving cattle, a groom of horses, dealing in four-footed beasts, butcher, brick-maker, smith.
♉	Tilling, planting, gardening, dealing in grain, four-footed beasts; or trades dealing in women's matters or women's running a household, soap-making, fulling.
♊	Clerk, mathematics, a bailiff collecting rents, surveying, as-tronomy, astrology, painting.
♋	(*Something pertaining to water*)[41]
♌	Serving-man, trades using fire, hunting, rider, coachman, smith, watchmaker, glassmaker.
♍	Secretary to an important person, schoolmaster, accountant, stationer or printer, politician, astrologer.
♎	Poet, orator, singer or musician, dealing in silk or linen, teaching children, bringing back captives.

---

[39] Abū Bakr Ch. II.12.4.

[40] *CA* II.84, pp. 450-51.

[41] **BD**: Lilly omits a special entry for this, but on p. 450 suggests fish and wa-terfowl.

♏	Surgeon, pharmacist, brazier or founder, brewer, vintner, waterman, maltster.
♐	Buying and selling cattle, chemistry, churchman, cook, baker.
♑	Candlemaker, smith, veterinarian of cattle, jeweler, farmer, wool-dealer, lead, or rural commodities, tilling.
♒	Ship's carpenter; if a planet aspects from a watery sign, a sailor, ship's master, trimmer, or painter, or a good merchant.
♓	Jester, singer, gambler, brewer, fish-monger.

I would like to mention my wife's chart in order to show you that some of these findings are accurate (Figure 11 above). In her chart, there are several planets in the 10th house and the Sun is in conjunction with the MC. It was not surprising that she has been busy in many different fields, and many of them matched the findings about professional significators in traditional texts.

As I mentioned before, the Mercury-Venus-Saturn conjunction in this chart indicates that my wife makes ornaments for women and sells them. She has also taught how to make these ornaments. Before setting up her own business, she worked as a teacher at an art school and taught jewelry-making, craft- and wood painting. When we set up our own business, she continued doing all of these and she still does.

Additionally, Aries is on the cusp of her 10th house and the Sun in Aries is close to the MC. Let's remember the professions Abū Bakr (via Lilly) associated with the fiery signs: blacksmiths, craftsmen (which Lilly specifies as including goldsmiths), bakers, and glass-makers. My wife was involved in silver- and goldsmithing as well as glass beadmaking between 2007 and 2015. She also gave lessons on these techniques. Mars, the lord of her 10th house, is in Taurus and in her 10th. According to Al-Bīrūnī, Mars in Taurus is related to the crafts of blacksmithing, glass, and also working in wood. Venus, the dispositor of Mars, is also in Taurus and in her 10th house, so it indicates wood (Mars) painting (Venus). Five planets are located in her 10th house in Taurus. According to William Lilly, the professional significator located in Taurus can indicate soap-making: my wife has been making healing soaps and selling them since 2015, and is still making ornaments and selling them just as Lilly and Abū Bakr noted (trades pertaining to women's matters). Again according to Lilly, Venus and Mars together indicate professions related to medicine and healing.[42] In her chart, Venus and Mars are not in conjunction, but they are in the same sign and Venus is the dispositor of Mars. Yes, my wife makes curative soaps.

Will the native be successful in his profession?

Traditional astrologers likewise evaluate this issue. If the professional significator is in its essential dignities, not afflicted by malefics, located in one of the strong houses (preferably in angles), eastern (but if Mercury and Venus, astronomically western), not burned or under the Sun's rays, in direct motion and fast, then the native can be successful in his profession. Lilly states that it's an indication that "the Native proves a famous workman, excellent and surmounting most of his Profession, that he shall gain great Estimation thereby, and be in public Reputation therefore."[43] On the other hand, if the professional significator is in detriment or fall, peregrine, or located in one of the cadent houses (especially the 6th and 12th), afflicted by malefics (that is, in conjunction, square, or opposition with Mars or Saturn, or a conjunction with the South Node), in retrograde motion, western (but if Venus and

---

[42] Lilly, *CA* III.149, p. 631.
[43] Lilly, *CA* III.149, p. 631.

Mercury, astronomically eastern), burned or under the Sun's rays, then the native may not be successful in his profession.

Firmicus states: "And so, generally we ought to know that whenever Mercury decrees the action, if he were adorned with the testimonies of the benevolent stars, he decrees glory, and the advancement of honors, and the trappings of greatest authority; but on the other hand the malevolent stars decree dejection, humiliations, miseries, and infamies; but in these decrees there is no little difference due to the nature of the stars."[44]

The significator being in hard aspects with malefics indicates that the native needs to work hard and sometimes his profession may be wasted and misused. Lilly makes some comments to this effect, based on which malefic afflicts the significator: "... when Saturn does afflict the significator, the native proves a sluggard, a lazy fellow, fearful to put himself forward. If Mars impede, the man is rash, obstinate, conceited, infamous: If both the infortunes at one time afflict the significator, then the afflictions he runs into by his profession are numberless, or have no end."[45]

Generally, malefics located in the Ascendant or MC bring damage and negativity in the profession, especially if they are contrary to the sect: Saturn in a nocturnal chart, and Mars in a diurnal chart.

Malefics located above the professional significator in a chart, or in the 10th house from the significator[46] also restricts profession progress. On the contrary, benefics located above the professional significator in a chart or in the 10th house from it bring advantages for the native's career.

---

[44] Firmicus Maternus, *Mathesis* IV.21. **BD**: For example, it makes a big difference whether the planet is Saturn or Mars.

[45] Lilly, *CA* III.149, p. 632.

[46] **BD**: That is, "overcoming" them. So if the professional significator is in Gemini, and a malefic is in Pisces (the tenth sign from Gemini), the malefic will overcome and harm the significator.

Concerning the universal professional significators, which are Mars, Venus, and Mercury, Abū 'Alī notes: "...if you found one in the Ascendant or the Midheaven, eastern, and having dignity there, and in a good aspect of the Sun or the Moon, it signifies the highness and usefulness of the mastery, and goodness, according to the nature of the planet which signifies this. Indeed, if none of these three were in the Ascendant or Midheaven, and some one of them were in the angle of the earth or in the seventh, the mastery will be less than that which I have said, with the alternating of labor and leisure."[47]

The house where the professional significator is located is very important. If the significator or the lord of the 10th house (which is the natural significator), is in one of the weak houses and afflicted, this is unfavorable in terms of career. The lord of the 10th house being located in the 12th house is also unfavorable. On this issue Morin says: "When the ruler of the tenth is in the twelfth, the profession of the native will be the cause of his misfortune, or he falls from it or loses it, which happened to me in the medical profession because Saturn was ruler of the tenth and in the twelfth. Or because of professional activities the native may be put in jail.[48]

Morin frequently uses his own chart and gives examples of it in his books. As you can see in his chart, Saturn the lord of the 10th house is in the 12th, peregrine and western.

---

[47] Al-Khayyāt, *JN* Ch. 33.
[48] Morin, p. 65.

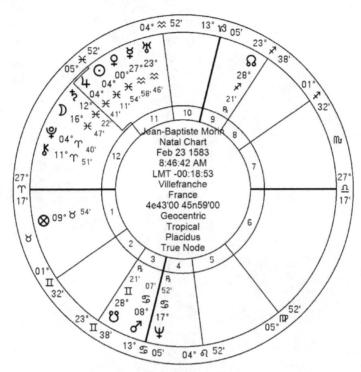

Figure 12: Jean-Baptiste Morin

He shares his knowledge and experience, saying: "But when the ruler of the twelfth is in the tenth, enemies, exile, prison, or misfortunes will be the cause of honor and preferment, as was the case with Cardinal Richelieu, whose Venus was ruler of the twelfth and in the MC, or within a close orb though actually located in the ninth."[49] Here is Cardinal Richelieu's chart (Figure 13):

[49] Morin, p. 65.

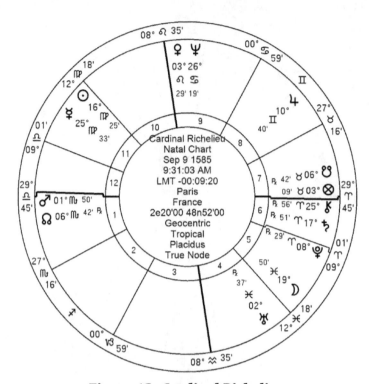

Figure 13: Cardinal Richelieu

Morin again gives an example from his own chart and tells: "And similarly, the ruler of the eleventh in the twelfth changes friends into enemies, which happened frequently to me; and the ruler of the twelfth in the eleventh causes the contrary. Likewise, when the ruler of the tenth is in the eleventh, the professional activities and repute of the native will bring him friends, while the ruler of the eleventh in the tenth foretells the reverse; and so on."[50]

Interpreting the 10th house, which is the house of career and profession, is crucial. According to modern astrologers, Capricorn is the natural sign of the 10th house while according to William Lilly Capricorn is only a co-significator of the 10th house.[51] Howev-

---

[50] Morin, p. 65.
[51] Lilly, *CA* III Ch. 7, p. 55.

er, modern astrologers claim that Saturn, the lord of Capricorn, is the natural significator of the 10th house. Here there is a conflict between traditional and modern astrology, because Saturn in the 10th house is not a favorable thing: it can cause the native to lose favor and have difficulties related to his career. Zoller notes: "Saturn's position in the 10th house is an indication of delays, hindrances, obstacles, problems, fall from grace, after having climbed very high up to get success."[52]

Of course, we need to evaluate Saturn in the 10th house in terms of dignities and debilities, his aspect with his lord, his lord's position, and other accidental dignities and debilities (being retrograde, burned, slow in motion, *etc.*). Morin states: "[Saturn] in fall in the tenth...makes the native sluggish and lazy, or indicates a mean occupation, or completely prevents honors and prestige or causes a fall from them, or brings disgrace upon the native. Saturn, however, would not cause such things if not in exile or fall in those places. Likewise, the ruler of the Ascendant or MC in exile[53] or fall bodes ill for the affairs of those houses."[54]

Let's see it in an example chart. In Al Pacino's nativity (Figure 14), Saturn is in Taurus in the 10th house, and is peregrine and burned. His lord Venus is in direct motion and fast, astrologically eastern and afflicted by Mars.

---

[52] Zoller, *Diploma* Lesson 6, p. 34.
[53] **BD**: In Morin, this means "detriment," such as the Sun in Aquarius.
[54] Morin, p. 75.

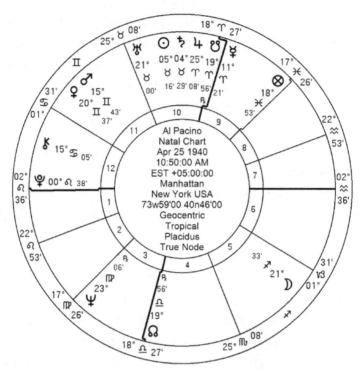

Figure 14: Al Pacino

The problem here is that Saturn is burned and afflicted due to the Venus-Mars conjunction. Saturn being closer to the cusp of the 10th than the Sun, indicates that native will face difficulties first and be restricted in professional matters; but after working hard he will find success later since the Sun, the planet of recognition and success, is farther from the MC than Saturn is. The Sun is both the lord of the Ascendant and victor of the MC, so he represents both the native and his profession. As the lord of the Ascendant the Sun's position will bring recognition in his later years although he will be restricted by Saturn when he is young. Morin says concerning the Sun, when he is the lord of the Ascendant and in the

10th house: "The Sun, ruler of the Ascendant and in the tenth house, raises the native to honors."[55]

Another quotation from Morin will help you understand this position better: "If the rulers of the first is in the tenth, or the ruler of the tenth in the first, professional activities, honors and prestige are indicated for the native in both cases; with the difference, however, that in the first case the native is stimulated by his own will and ambition and works with industry to attain recognition or an important position, while in the second case he does not strive thus, but honor and preferment will come to him quite without expectation."[56]

As we learned about what the lord of the 1st in the 10th indicates, and the lord of the 10th in the 1st, let me show you another chart. Below (Figure 15), you will see the chart of a famous Turkish actress, Hülya Avşar.[57] In addition to her being crowned Miss Turkey, she worked as a movie actress, singer, stage actress, TV show hostess, and she had a magazine named after her.

Mercury, the lord of her 10th house, is located in her 1st house and Virgo where he rules by domicile, exaltation, and face. Having made first place in the "Branded Celebrities Survey," Avşar has been very successful in her career for many years. Here we see that the rule works well: a planet in its own domicile brings persistence and stability in the issues represented by the houses it rules. Morin explains this particular situation as follows: "The same planet ruling the Ascendant and the MC promises recognition in professional activities."[58]

---

[55] Morin, p. 56.
[56] Morin, p. 63.
[57] https://en.wikipedia.org/wiki/Hülya_Avşar.
[58] Morin, p. 69.

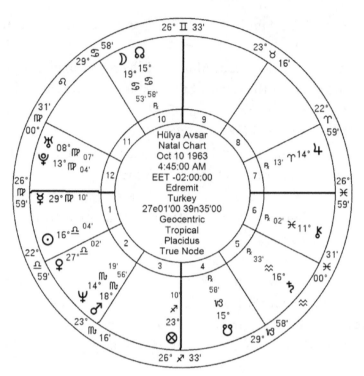

Figure 15: Hülya Avşar

The lord of the 10th house being located in the 10th contributes to the realization of 10th-house issues, and even if it is Mars or Saturn it may bring success when dignified. In Figure 16 (Ezel Akay), the lord of the MC is Saturn, who conjoins with the MC in Capricorn, a sign he rules. Saturn is eastern of the Sun, in conjunction with Jupiter, and is not afflicted by the other malefic Mars. He is under the Sun's rays but not burned. He makes a sextile with the Moon, and is direct in motion and fast. The native has been an actor but is well known as a producer where he proved successful. Although he has been faced with great difficulties and sometimes risked losing favor, he survived. He has been successful in his career in general and has produced movies in cooperation with foreigners (Saturn, the lord of the MC, is also the lord of the 9th house and in conjunction with Jupiter, a planet in the 9th).

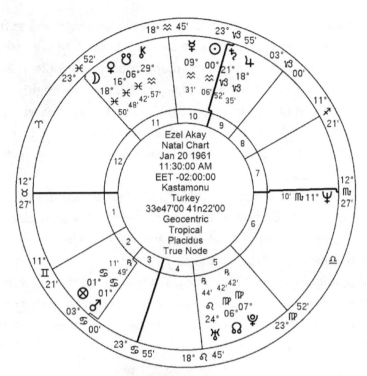

Figure 16: Ezel Akay

Professional significators having supportive aspects or mutual reception with benefics, even by square or opposition, increase the chances for professional success because benefics are aligned with success and prestige. Of course, it is not only the support of Venus and Jupiter that indicates success: supportive aspects of other planets also increase the chances for success, or make it easier to have. Abū ʿAlī notes: "If [the significator] were of good condition and in a good place, and Mercury looked at it by a lucky aspect, it signifies the native has a good mastery and riches, and will profit in his business, and [will be involved] in the knowledge of writing and arithmetic, giving many things and taking many things, with good skill and endowed with honest morals."[59] He goes on to say

---

[59] Al-Khayyāt, *JN* Ch. 33.

that if Saturn aspects with friendly rays, the livelihood will be from the cultivation of lands and from settling them; if Jupiter, he will be a writer and orator, honored among important people; if Mars, he will be a physician or seer, sharp and having foresight; if the Sun aspected it or was with it, he will be a high master, a writer for kings, and valued among them, with a noble mastery and teaching; if the Moon, it signifies the native's knowledge, teaching, fortune, and perfection.

Generally speaking, when the professional significator is on the cusp of the 10th house, the lord of the 10th house is placed in the 10th, and the majority of these are in fixed signs, it indicates that the native will be stubborn in his career, will prefer continuity, and not change jobs often. These are important factors for reaching professional success. The professional significator or the lord of the 10th house being located in the sign it rules, indicates a successful career life.

When will success come?

As the Sun represents recognition and success, it is suggested that we treat him as an Ascendant. According to 'Umar al-Tabarī, the Sun's natal position should be considered: if he is in an eastern quadrant, the native obtains nobility and prestige in his profession at an early age; if in a western quadrant, at a later age (if the natal chart promises success, of course). Likewise, we may consider the Sun's triplicity lords to determine when the native will reach success in his career. If all three of these lords are strongly placed, then the native reaches success at an early age; but the native will have difficulties in being successful in his career if all three of these triplicity lords are weakly placed.[60] He may not even have a good reputation.

---

[60] Al-Tabarī, *TBN* III.9.

As for the timing of success, we may also have a look at the lord of the sign where the professional significator or the lord of the 10th is located. If the significator itself is not in a good position but its lord is favorably placed, then the native obtains success in the later years of his life. If the significator is favorably placed but its lord is not, then the native becomes successful in his early years but it decreases in later years. Dispositors are important in determining the timing.

In order to predict when success will come, we may also see when the professional significator becomes the lord of the *firdaria* period, or through profections we may see when the profected Ascendant reaches the house where it is placed. If success in that period is also confirmed through the solar return chart, then we may be confident about the timing of success.

Let's practice these ideas on Hülya Avşar's chart (Figure 15). To start with, we see that the Sun is in the western quarter of her chart. This means it may take time to gain recognition. In fact, she was recognized in earlier years: she was Miss Turkey in a beauty contest, but her crown was taken away as she was married. However, only a short time after this contest, she became popular in the movie industry and has rapidly started climbing up the celebrity ladder.

We obtain accurate results by looking at the Sun's triplicity lords; let me briefly give some details on this method. The triplicity lords of airy signs (where the Sun is) are Saturn, Mercury, and lastly Jupiter; but for nocturnal charts (as in this case) the lords follow this order: Mercury, Saturn, Jupiter. Each planet in this order represents the one-third of the native's life, roughly 25 years apiece. In her chart, the first triplicity lord Mercury is the most strongly-placed planet in the chart: he is powerfully placed in Virgo and not afflicted, indicating that she will achieve success in her early ages (between ages 0-25), and she will do this through her personal skills and her physical appearance, as Mercury is in the 1st house and very close to the Ascendant. The other triplicity lords, Saturn and Jupiter, are also powerfully placed. Saturn is in his domicile and triplicity, and placed in the 5th house, which is a strong, succeedent house. The Saturn-Mars square indicates that the period between the ages of 25-50 (ruled by Saturn) will be relatively challenging. Jupiter, the third triplicity lord, is in Aries, in his own triplicity, and strongly placed in an angular house. As he is retrograde we may expect some delays and dissatisfactions, but as he is strongly placed he brings recognition and success in the last one-third of her life. Jupiter is not afflicted by the malefics and his lord Mars is in a strong position in Scorpio. We get the same results if we take the triplicity lords of the 10th house, because Gemini is also an airy sign.

As the domicile lord of the 10th, Mercury's position in the 1st indicates that the native will achieve success in her early years because the quarter between the Ascendant and Midheaven represents the earliest period of life. In fact, although we generally consider only the arc between the degree of the Ascendant and Midheaven, I also include the space enclosed by the 1st house, especially when there is a planet very close to the Ascendant and in the same sign with it (which in whole signs is also considered the 1st house because it is the first sign).

Here I would like to remind you that this is a nocturnal chart, and so we should also consider the Moon. The Moon is placed in her domicile which is Cancer, and in the 10th house. She also has triplicity lordship here. The Moon-North Node conjunction increases her power. The Moon's aspects with the Sun and Jupiter simultaneously signify that the native will get recognition and achieve success and prestige.

By profection of the Ascendant, the native's prospects will increase when we reach the 10th house or the lord of the 10th: in this chart that means the 10th and the 1st houses. Mercury, the lord of these houses, is strongly placed, not afflicted, and promises success. We reach the 10th and 1st in order when the native is 21 and 24, 33 and 36, 45 and 48, 57 and 60, 69 and 72, *etc*. Her prospects will be higher in her 10th house profection. Due to the Moon and North Node being in the 10th house, this position enhances the native's potential as a female figure to gain social recognition, achievement, and respect.

Similarly, we may also expect success when the profection reaches the Sun. Here the Sun is placed in the 1st house but close to the cusp of the 2nd, and Venus (his and its lord) is one of the most powerful planets of the chart. Venus is also important because she makes a trine to the MC and is also the professional significator. Consequently, when the native is 25, 37, 49, 61, and 73 years old (the profection of the Ascendant to the 2nd house, and the location of Venus), so that Venus is the lord of the year, the native will also have a chance for professional success. Periodical transits and progressions of Venus will also be helpful. Positive and supportive transits will bring success easily, whereas negative and difficult aspects will be challenging.

Through the *firdaria* we may also consider the periods when Mercury, the Sun, or Venus is the lord. In the table below you may see when these planets will be the main *firdaria* lord as well as the sub-lord. During such times, the transits and progressions the lords get will provide information about the native reaching success easily or with difficulty.

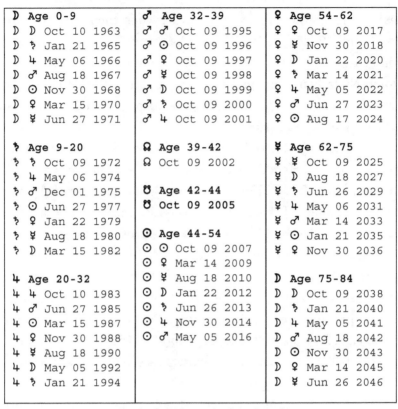

☽ Age 0-9	♂ Age 32-39	♀ Age 54-62
☽ ☽ Oct 10 1963	♂ ♂ Oct 09 1995	♀ ♀ Oct 09 2017
☽ ♄ Jan 21 1965	♂ ☉ Oct 09 1996	♀ ☿ Nov 30 2018
☽ ♃ May 06 1966	♂ ♀ Oct 09 1997	♀ ☽ Jan 22 2020
☽ ♂ Aug 18 1967	♂ ☿ Oct 09 1998	♀ ♄ Mar 14 2021
☽ ☉ Nov 30 1968	♂ ☽ Oct 09 1999	♀ ♃ May 05 2022
☽ ♀ Mar 15 1970	♂ ♄ Oct 09 2000	♀ ♂ Jun 27 2023
☽ ☿ Jun 27 1971	♂ ♃ Oct 09 2001	♀ ☉ Aug 17 2024
♄ Age 9-20	☊ Age 39-42	☿ Age 62-75
♄ ♄ Oct 09 1972	☊ Oct 09 2002	☿ ☿ Oct 09 2025
♄ ♃ May 06 1974		☿ ☽ Aug 18 2027
♄ ♂ Dec 01 1975	☋ Age 42-44	☿ ♄ Jun 26 2029
♄ ☉ Jun 27 1977	☋ Oct 09 2005	☿ ♃ May 06 2031
♄ ♀ Jan 22 1979		☿ ♂ Mar 14 2033
♄ ☿ Aug 18 1980	☉ Age 44-54	☿ ☉ Jan 21 2035
♄ ☽ Mar 15 1982	☉ ☉ Oct 09 2007	☿ ♀ Nov 30 2036
	☉ ♀ Mar 14 2009	
♃ Age 20-32	☉ ☿ Aug 18 2010	☽ Age 75-84
♃ ♃ Oct 10 1983	☉ ☽ Jan 22 2012	☽ ☽ Oct 09 2038
♃ ♂ Jun 27 1985	☉ ♄ Jun 26 2013	☽ ♄ Jan 21 2040
♃ ☉ Mar 15 1987	☉ ♃ Nov 30 2014	☽ ♃ May 05 2041
♃ ♀ Nov 30 1988	☉ ♂ May 05 2016	☽ ♂ Aug 18 2042
♃ ☿ Aug 18 1990		☽ ☉ Nov 30 2043
♃ ☽ May 05 1992		☽ ♀ Mar 14 2045
♃ ♄ Jan 21 1994		☽ ☿ Jun 26 2046

Figure 17: Firdaria periods of Hülya Avşar

2: HOW DO I WORK?

Up to now, we have read what the ancient astrologers stated. Now I would like to make my own remarks and summary by telling you how I find the significator of the profession. I generally use a quadrant house system while sometimes referring to whole-sign houses. The first thing I consider is the Ascendant. If there is no planet in it, I look at the 10th house to see if any planet is in it. If not, I look at the 7th in the same way; if none is in it, I consider the 4th. According to traditional rules, when planets are in the angular houses we should give priority to the three universal significators: Mercury, Venus, and Mars. While I do give priority to these three, I do prefer considering the other planets in the angular houses, including the Sun and the Moon: by "other planets" I include Uranus, Neptune, and Pluto, in addition to Jupiter and Saturn. There are numerous professions today as compared with ancient times, so we may discover many professions that are related to the impersonal planets.

After writing down the planets in angular houses, I review the planets which are eastern of the Sun. If Mars, Jupiter, or Saturn rise before the Sun, I consider them eastern; if Mercury and Venus rise after the Sun I consider them eastern (although astronomically they are western). I regard a waxing Moon as eastern and a waning Moon as western. I note the planets which are in angular houses and also eastern: if there are any, I note the one which aspects both the Sun and Moon, no matter whether it is eastern or western. I also consider the planets which are both eastern of the Sun and western of the Moon, whether or not they aspect the luminaries.

In the next step, I address the sign on the MC and I pay attention to the nature, element, and quality of this sign. For example, if Leo is on the MC I think that the native may be involved in administrative affairs or do his own business; if Libra, the native may be involved in the arts or legal affairs; if Gemini, I think the native may possibly be an author, teacher, or public relations expert.

Then I pay attention to the nature of the lord of the MC, and the nature of the sign and house it is in. For me, the nature of the lord of the MC is important. For example, if the lord of the MC is Venus and she is in the 5th house, then I think that the native is involved in artistic professions; but if it is Mars and he is in the 5th, I think about professions related to sports. The sign that the lord of the MC is located in gives us information about the native's profession and also how he carries it out. For me, the lord of the MC is an important possible significator of the profession, even it is unfavorably placed or afflicted.

Next I analyze the planets which aspect the MC and its lord. A dignified planet which aspects the MC and is favorably placed in the chart affects the native's professional tendencies and talents. Planets which aspect the lord of the MC are also important in determining the native's professional talents.

Then, based on the chart being diurnal or nocturnal, I find the planet that the Moon first aspects after the pre-natal New or Full Moon (diurnal chart), or the planet that the natal Moon first aspects (nocturnal chart), or the planets that aspect the Lot of Fortune (nocturnal chart). In a nocturnal chart, if the planet that the Moon will aspect first also aspects the Lot, I focus on this planet.

Next I deal with the professional significator and its lord. I consider the sign and house in which the significator is located, and its aspects. The sign where the significator is located may indicate the native's professional tendencies and talents.

I also think we should consider the 2nd and 6th houses. The 2nd is related to the native's earnings and possessions, so it should be related to his profession. The 6th is also related to the native's daily routine, work environment, and skills. So, the planets located in these houses may indicate the profession, especially if they aspect the MC. The 6th house represents the native's employees and his relations with them, but also rules the native's working capacity, desire, and ability to serve others and his skills. Let me give an example from my own chart (see below). My Mars and Saturn are located in the 6th house and in one angle of the T-square aspect pattern (Mars-Saturn, Pluto-Uranus, and Jupiter). I work really hard. People around me tell that they have never seen someone as busy as I am. I think this is because of Mars and Saturn in the 6th house. Yes, I had some problems with employees but these problems mostly arose because of their own problems. I believe I have always been soft-hearted and selfless towards them. The reason for this is Pisces in the 6th house. As an example, in 2001 I came to the brink of bankruptcy because I did not want to fire any of my employees.

Now, we may also use this chart to determine the professional significator. There is only one planet in the angular houses: Venus. So, I write her down as a possible significator of the profession. When I look for the eastern planets, I first see Mercury (again, he is astronomically western but as an inferior planet we can call him eastern). Uranus and Pluto are also eastern. I write them down, too.

As this is a nocturnal chart, I have a look at the Moon's first aspect: she applies to a square with Mercury. Mercury, being western of the Moon, also makes an aspect with the Lot of Fortune: I note Mercury. On the other hand, the Sun is applying to the Lot of Fortune, so I also note the Sun.

Cancer is on the MC. Her lord the Moon, in Scorpio and the 3rd house (but 2nd sign), is the natural significator of the profession because the MC pertains to that. As the Moon is in the second sign, which is also a financial sign, she is important. So, I note the Moon. Then I look at the planets that aspect the MC and I see only Mercury: again, I write him down.

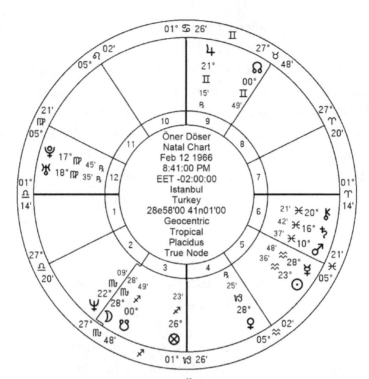

Figure 18: Öner Döşer

The Lot of profession is at 13° Gemini, in the 9th house, indicating professions which are suitable for Gemini. I again write down Mercury, the lord of the Lot.

Mercury attracts my attention as he is a repeating significator. Mercury is in contact with both the Sun and the Moon, eastern of the Sun, western of the Moon, in his triplicity in Aquarius, in a supportive trine with the benefic Jupiter, is not afflicted by malefics, but only burned. He is also direct and fast. So, I determine Mercury as the professional significator. (On the other hand, the other significator, Venus, is still prominent.)

Let me tell you a little bit about my professional life. For 20 years, I worked at my family's stores. First I helped my father, and then after his death I alone managed the family stores between 1997 and 2003. The prominent Venus in the 4th house of my chart indicates a family business. Additionally, Cancer is on the cusp of my 10th house, indicating family business again. Venus is a triplicity lord of Cancer on the MC. Moreover, Venus is in sextile with the Moon the lord of the MC. Our stores were in Istanbul's Grand Bazaar, where we used to sell goods for women and souvenirs for 20 years. My grandfather was the first owner of these stores, where he continued his profession connected with furniture and upholstery (which fits Venus's nature). As my chart is a nocturnal one, the aspects of the Moon are more important. The Moon separates from a sextile with Venus and applies to a square with Mercury. This means: professions of a Venusian nature appear in the first years of life, and then professions of a Mercurial nature come later. This was the fact really, since I have been a professional astrologer since I left the family business in 2003. Mercury, who is my professional significator, is the lord of the 9th house: for the last 15 years I have been working as a teacher, author, and consultant in astrology; I started the School of Astrology in 2005, as well as our publishing house, where we published nearly twenty books by 2011; also Astrology TV, which broadcasts online, in 2012. I am still in the trade business because we have an online shop where we sell the ornaments my wife makes (as Venus is placed in the 10th from the 7th, which indicates the professional activities of my wife).

Mercury, my professional significator, makes a conjunction with the Sun, a square with the Moon, and a trine with Jupiter. I worked with my father (Mercury-Sun conjunction), we became partners in 1994 and worked as partners until his death in 1997. I was involved in the family business (Mercury-Moon square) and it was all about women (women's bags, ornaments, etc.), since 2003 I have been teaching, writing, and consulting (Mercury-Jupiter trine), and it has been the most enjoyable thing I have done up to now (trine). In his course, Robert Zoller says: "I have seen many instances of 5th house Financial Significators where the native has his or her own business, which produces wealth by itself. Yet because he or she has a splendid 5th house Financial Significator, the native stands to inherit family money as well."[1] That's true for me: I always had my own business. Although at first I inherited a business from my family, later I did something which was totally different from this family business.

Additionally, astrology was just a hobby when I started to learn it (5th house), but later it became a full-time professional practice.

At this juncture I would like to mention what my teacher Robert Zoller, from whom I learned mundane astrology in 2004, advised me during a consultation with him. As Mars, the lord of my 7th house, was in the 6th house and in conjunction with Saturn, he advised me not to set up partnerships. Mars was in a weak position and problematic and he was in the 6th house, which is the 12th house of the 7th. Zoller told me: "Your partner may be sick or pull your leg. I advise you not to set up partnership with others; however, you may work with your wife, because Venus in your 4th house makes a sextile with the Moon." As I mentioned before, Venus located in the 10th house from the 7th house is related to my wife's profession, which is of Venus's nature. Additionally, the Moon rules my 10th house. The harmonious sextile between these two indicates that being in a professional partnership with my wife would be beneficial for me. Zoller also told me that I should be careful with my business, and avoid businesses which require employing too many people. While I was manufacturing women's bags between 1996 and 2002, I had difficulties because of my employees. My partner and I had 20 employees in our shop, and we came to the brink of bankruptcy as I could barely provide for their expenses and needs. Zoller had one more piece of advice: "Don't do business with your friend!" The reason for this warning was the

---

[1] Zoller, *Diploma* Lesson 13, p. 23.

square between the Sun, the lord of my 11th house, and the Moon, the lord of the MC.

Let's get back to our main subject. After determining the possible significator of the profession, I choose the one which repeats and which is the strongest one. By the planets which this planet makes aspects with, I make predictions and give advice about the native's probable profession and professional skills.

For me, the placement of the lord of the MC is very important. The house position of this planet, and of course its aspects with other planets, give key information about the field of life where the native reveals his professional skills. I also consider the houses ruled by any planets in the 10th: those house topics indicate fields of life that the native's profession is related to. The Sun's position in the chart is also important. The Sun is a natural significator of recognition, and the native may be recognized through his professional skills.

At this point, some practice on example charts will be useful.

3: EXAMPLE CHARTS

In Diana Ross's chart Mercury, the lord of the MC, is located in the 5th house. We know her profession is related to the arts and entertainment sector. The Mercury-Jupiter trine brings recognition in this area and reaching great masses of people in the international arena (Jupiter in the 9th house). On the other hand, the Sun may also signify the fields in which the native will get recognition, especially when he is in dignity and makes favorable aspects, and is in aspect with the MC. We should also consider the planets which the Sun aspects because they may indicate the native's talents. Below you may see her chart:

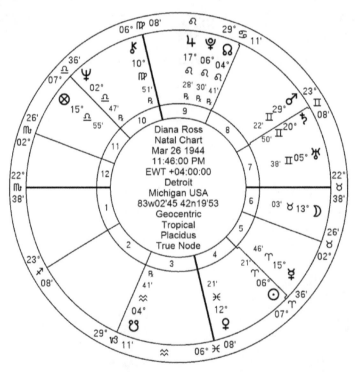

Figure 19: Diana Ross

We should consider the houses ruled by planets in the MC, because these houses indicate the fields in which the native shows
his talents to society, and the skills he uses. In Antonio Banderas's
chart Jupiter, the exalted lord of the 5th house, is in the 10th house,
bringing recognition in artistic fields.

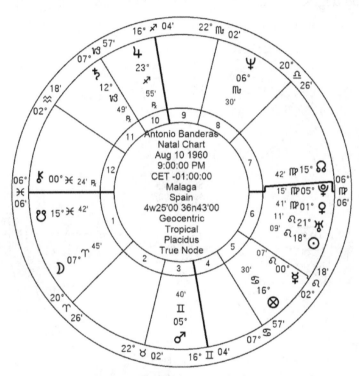

Figure 20: Antonio Banderas

Jupiter rules the degree of Banderas's Ascendant. So, Jupiter in
the 10th combines the native (Pisces) with the 5th house (Cancer).
Jupiter being in his domicile in Sagittarius, and his trine with the
Sun, indicate recognition. The Sun (who is in his own triplicity) is
one of the triplicity lords of the MC itself and aspects the MC, although he is in a cadent house in the 6th. Jupiter empowers him
through his aspect to the Sun from the 10th house: so, he increases
the chances for recognition.

We are told that planets close to the degree of the Ascendant indicate the native's profession or his professional skills. In Pope Benedict XVI's chart, Jupiter close to the Ascendant indicates his tendencies towards religious issues. Being the lord of the 9th house, Jupiter indicates a religious personality here. He also has dignity in the degree of the MC. So, issues related to the 9th house contribute to the native's profession.

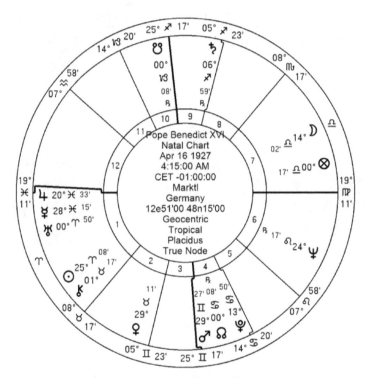

Figure 21: Pope Benedict XVI

Now, let's consider the chart of the astronomer and astrological writer al-Bīrūnī. In his chart, Mercury is eastern of the Sun and is the lord of both the Ascendant and MC. This signifies that al-Bīrūnī will be known for Mercurial subjects. Although he is burned, Mercury is getting stronger as he separates from the Sun and is in his dignity in Virgo—in addition to the strength of his location in the 1st house. On the other hand, as this is a nocturnal chart, the planet which the Moon will aspect first is also important for us. The Moon is applying to a sextile with Saturn: Saturn is related to scientific works, and is the lord of the 5th house of this chart, which is related to creativity.

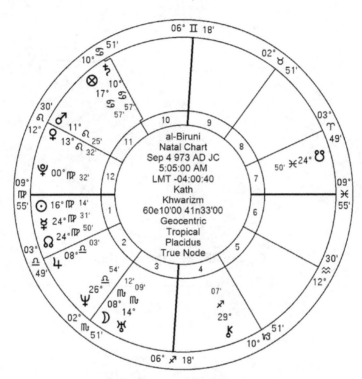

Figure 22: Al-Bīrūnī

In Brooke Shields's chart the Moon and Venus are the nearest planets to the MC. This indicates that the actress will get public recognition and will stand out with her beauty. Venus is related to artistic fields like acting and modeling.

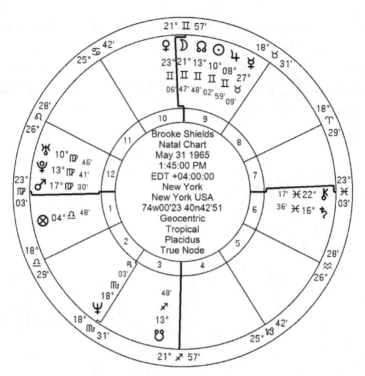

Figure 23: Brooke Shields

4: TRADITIONAL ASTROLOGERS ON PROFESSIONAL SIGNIFICATORS

In this chapter I would like to share with you my compilation of professions suggested for each planet based on the books of the traditional astrologers. The universal significators (Mercury, Venus, Mars) take priority, and the others follow.

Mercury as the significator

Ptolemy:[1] Writers, businessmen, calculators, teachers, bankers, soothsayers, astrologers, sacrificers, and people who handle documents and engage in interpretation.

Firmicus Maternus:[2] "He makes either kings or those put in charge of judges, or those entrusted with the royal accounts, or the teachers of emperors, or he decrees actions like these in every way according to the nature of the signs, and the powers of those who supply testimony to him. He even makes orators, chief physicians, mathematicians, astrologers, *haruspices*, but decrees these things according to the power of the signs. For, being established in the solid signs he decrees the greatest judgments and reasonings; but if he were found in the tropical signs, he decrees duties due to changes[3] or interpretations; being put in the equinoctial signs he is in charge of public weights [and standards]; but being found in the double signs he decrees clever, ingenious people, inventors, astrologers, and all which seem to be like these arts and teachings in this manner."

Al-Tabarī:[4] Scribe, astrologer, arithmetician.

---

[1] **BD**: All summaries of Ptolemy are taken from *Tet.* IV.4 (Robbins pp. 383-87).

[2] **BD**: All quotations from Firmicus are taken from *Mathesis* IV.21.

[3] *Mutationes*. **BD**: This can refer to changes in law or the constitution.

[4] Al-Tabarī, *TBN* III.9.

Al-Qabīsī:[5] Making distinctions, public address, rhetoric, activities which arise in mathematics like business, calculation, geometry, philosophy, taking omens, sorcery, writing, poetry.

Al-Bīrūnī:[6] Merchants, calculators and surveyors, astrologers, necromancers and fortune-tellers, geometrician, philosopher, disputation, poetry, eloquence, manual dexterity and anxiety for perfection in everything, selling slaves, hides, books, coins, profession of barber, manufacture of combs.

Schoener:[7] Teacher, one who does computations, merchant, one who knows and discovers things, judging the power of the stars, and generally engaged in the reading and exposition of books.

Lilly, CA III:[8] Trades that deal more with the mind than the body: letters, numbers, writing, learning, eloquence, arithmetic, astrology, philosophical speculations, merchandise, poetry, inventing mechanisms (but if Mercury is not in a good aspect with Jupiter, the native may profit little by these).

Lilly, CA I:[9] Literary men, philosophers, mathematicians, astrologers, merchants, secretaries, scriveners, diviners, sculptors, poets, orators, lawyers, schoolmasters, stationers, printers, money-changers, attorneys, ambassadors, commissioners, clerks, inventor, accountants, thieves, prattling muddy ministers, busy secretaries (and unlearned), grammarians, tailors, deliverymen, messengers, footmen, lending money with interest.

---

[5] Al-Qabīsī, Ch. II.31.
[6] **BD**: All material from al-Bīrūnī come from his §435.
[7] Schoener I.11, **9**.
[8] See *CA* I.13, p. 78.
[9] See *CA* I.149, p. 627.

Venus as the significator

Ptolemy: Those who manufacture or trade in flowers, oint-ments, wine, colors, dyes, spices, jewelry and adornments, medical drugs, clothing.

Firmicus Maternus: "She will make goldsmiths, gold-platers, workers in gold leaf, silversmiths, musicians, organ players, paint-ers. But if she were found in the cast-down and lazy places,[10] she will make entertainers, fast-food vendors, shopkeepers,[11] perfum-ers, and who tend to sell crowns made of a variety of flowers on festival and sacred days, and whatever things are necessary for happiness or pleasure."

Al-Qabīsī:[12] Those involving musical instruments, adornment, pretty forms, playing backgammon and chess, dancing, idleness, adultery, whores, the children of adultery, sexual intercourse and much lesbianism and hiring <prostitutes> , the arrangement of garlands, wearing of crowns, cleanliness, clothing, ornaments, gold and silver, showing off, love of amusement, laughter, joy, per-fumes, scents, fermented drinks, tranquility of mind towards everyone, generosity, friendliness, passionate love, flirtation, houses of worship, and adherence to religion. It indicates engage-ment with the craft of melodies at the level of song and other things.

Al-Bīrūnī: Works of beauty and magnificence, fond of bazaars, commerce, measuring by weight, length and bulk; dealing in pic-tures and colors, goldsmith work, tailoring, manufacturing perfumes, dealing in pearls, gold and silver ornaments, musk, white and green clothes, maker of crowns and diadems, accompa-

---

[10] **BD**: In Firmicus this refers to the signs of houses in aversion to the As-cendant: the second, sixth, eighth, and twelfth.
[11] **BD**: "Entertainers" and "shopkeepers" here also connote restaurants and bars or taverns, and probably innkeepers.
[12] Al-Qabīsī, Ch. II.25.

nying singing, composing songs, playing the lute, feasts, games and gaming.

Schoener:[13] The native will associate himself with works of outward appearances, aromatic and good-smelling things, painting, the dying and weaving of fabrics, or trade in things that have to do with fragrances, such as the essence of flowers, etc.

Lilly, CA III:[14] Pharmacists, grocers, perfumers, vintners, those dealing in provisions, painters, jewelers, painters, tire-makers, wardrobe-keepers, musicians.

Lilly, CA I:[15] Musicians, gamblers, silk-men, dealers in textiles, linen-drapers, painters, jewelers, players, working with fine stones, embroiderers, women-tailors, choristers, fiddlers, pipers; when joined with the Moon, ballad singers, perfumers, seamstresses, picture-drawers, engravers, upholsterers, painters, glovers, those selling commodities which adorn women (including for the face).

Mars as the significator

Ptolemy: If configured with the Sun: those who use fire (cooks, smiths, miners, etc.). If not configured with the Sun, then those working with iron, shipbuilders, carpenters, farmers, and all of their subordinate laborers.

Firmicus Maternus: "He makes brilliant and noble arts from fire or from iron."

Al-Qabīsī:[16] Every profession involving fire, or what is done with iron, such as beating with hammers and pressing out swords.

Al-Bīrūnī: Law-making, selling and making armor, blacksmith's craft, grooms, shepherds, butchers, veterinary surgeons, circumcisers, sellers of hounds, cheetahs, boars, wolves, copper, sickles,

---

[13] Schoener I.11, **13**.
[14] See *CA* III.149, p. 628.
[15] See *CA* I.12, pp. 74-75.
[16] Al-Qabīsī, Ch. II.13.

beer, glass, boxes, wooden cups, brigandage, contention, house-breaking, highwaymen, grave-robbers and prison, torture, execution.

Schoener:[17] If he has an aspect with the Sun, a kindler of fire; if in a good state then a miner of gold or goldsmith; if in a bad state, the kindler of an oven.

Lilly, CA III:[18] Professions involving bodily strength and especially manual trades, full of toil and using fire.

Lilly, CA I:[19] Soldiers and military officers, physicians, pharmacists, surgeons, alchemists, gunners, butchers, marshals, sergeants, bailiffs, hangmen, thieves, smiths, bakers, armorers, watchmakers, tailors, dealers in swords and knives, barbers, dyers, cooks, carpenters, gamblers, bear-keepers, tanners, curriers.

Jupiter as the significator

Al-Qabīsī:[20] Involvement in religious law, such as judging, passing sentences, reconciliation between people, and spreading the good.

Al-Bīrūnī: Noble actions, good government, religion doing good, interpretation of dreams; goldsmiths' work, banking; selling old gold and silver, white clothes, grapes and sugar-cane.

Lilly, CA I:[21] Judges, senators, councilors, religious figures and officials, chancellors, doctors of the civil law, scholars and students in a university or college, lawyers, clothiers, wool-drapers.

---

[17] Schoener I.11, **15**.
[18] See *CA* III.149, p. 629.
[19] See *CA* I.10, p. 67.
[20] Al-Qabīsī, Ch. II.8.
[21] See *CA* I.9, p. 63.

Saturn as the significator

Al-Qabīsī:[22] Of professions it has noble activities involving water, like cultivation and management of lands and rivers when it is fortunate; but vile activities when it is harmed, like massage in baths, the occupations of fulling, navigation and serving drinks.

Al-Bīrūnī: Building, paymaster, farming, reclaiming land and distribution of water, apportioning money and heritages, grave-digging; selling things made of iron, lead, bone, hair; copper, black slaves; knowledge used for bad purposes, such acts of the government as lead to evil oppression, wrath, captivity, torture.

Lilly, CA I:[23] Leather-dyers, sewage workers,[24] miners, tinners, potters, broom-men, plumbers, brick-makers, chimney-sweepers, Church sextons,[25] bearers of dead corpses, scavengers, hostlers,[26] coal-dealers, carters, gardeners, ditch diggers, candlemakers, dyers of black cloth, herdsman, shepherd, or cow-keeper.

The Sun as the significator

Al-Qabīsī:[27] It has ruling leadership, shooting, arrows and hunting, and all kinds of cleaning of bodies, inside and out.

Al-Bīrūnī: Receiving, giving, and selling gold brocades.

Zoller:[28] Positions of power, dignity, authority and responsibility, goldsmiths, gilders, those who work with or sell gold,

---

[22] Al-Qabīsī, Ch. II.2.

[23] See *CA* I.8, p. 59.

[24] **BD**: Lilly says "night-farmers," which I take to be a euphemism for outhouse cleaners (as also in the English "night soil").

[25] **BD**: Sextons do a lot of the caretaking and "grunt work" in a church, including burying the dead.

[26] **BD**: This refers to people who manage and take care of horses, vehicles, and machines when not in use.

[27] Al-Qabīsī, Ch. II.18.

[28] Zoller, *Diploma* Lesson 12 p. 27.

artists, models, actors, salesmen, courtiers, noblemen, kings, princes, emperors, TV announcers, newscasters, performers.

Lilly, CA I:[29] Powerful, governmental people, constables and sheriffs, local magistrates, goldsmiths, brass-workers, pewterers, coppersmiths, minters of money.

The Moon as the significator

Al-Qabīsī:[30] The post, messages, disclosures, opening up of lands, and activities concerning water.

Al-Bīrūnī: Those engaged in business matters, missions, agencies, accounting, strenuous in religion and divine law, skill in all branches; practice of medicine, geometry, the higher sciences, measuring land and water; growing and cutting hair; selling food, silver rings and virgins, also indicates captivity and prison for the deceptions of wizards.

Zoller:[31] Sailors, travelers, fishermen, those who manage public conveyances (transit authority), dealers in fluids, nurses, midwives, maids, all common employments, hypnotists, those who exploit images in the mind, divination, especially by crystal balls or hydromancy, oracles, witches. Visionaries.

Lilly, CA I:[32] Female powerful people and ladies; the common people; travelers, pilgrims, sailors, fishermen and fisherwomen, fishmongers, brewers, bartenders, vintners, letter-carriers, coachmen, huntsmen, messengers, navigators, millers, alewives, maltsters, drunkards, oyster wives, charwomen, and generally such women as carry commodities in the streets, as also midwives, nurses; men with carriages for hire, boatmen, water-bearers.

---

[29] See *CA* I.11, p. 71.
[30] Al-Qabīsī, Ch. II.36.
[31] Zoller, *Diploma* Lesson 12 p. 27.
[32] See *CA* I.14, p. 81.

5: PLANETS AND PROFESSIONS

To help you make predictions based on the professional significators, you may also take note of some of the professions assigned to the planets in the list below.

Moon
Hotel-keeper, landlord, landscaper, public relations expert, money-lender, housekeeper, healer, businessman in the food industry, sailor, fisherman, sea-products salesman, retailer, people who are involved in jobs more typical for women, babysitter, real estate agent, photographer, cleaner, psychic, peddler, social worker, cook, catering workers, hotel personnel, fortune-teller, farmer, gourmet, illustrator.

Mercury
Researcher, astronomer, astrologer, mathematician, communications professions, editor, author, preacher, translator, linguist, teacher, accountant, lawyer, expert in analytics, software engineer, inspector, transporter, postman, publisher, salesman, merchant, distributor, grocer, journalist, news agent, courier, interviewer, secretary, commentator, computer programmer, philosopher, animal trainer, juggler, magician, chemist, architect, travel agent, traveler, historian, man of letters, marketing expert, sales clerk, artisan, advertiser, consultant, airline personnel, middleman, announcer, graphic designer.

Venus
Actor and actress, artist, musician, designer, architect, interior design, landscape architect, entertainment industry, fashion model, professions related to fashion and luxury, tailor, draper, gardener, florist, dancer, beautician, people who sell women's apparel, cur-

tain seller, jeweler, photographer, public relations expert, cosmetics and cosmetology, pianist, poet, comedian, textile supplier, sculptor, furniture maker, gambling, opera singer (and other singers), painter.

Sun

Political leader, executive, bureaucrat, politician, foreman, organizer, actor or actress, performer, supervisor, athlete, cardiologist, jeweler, animator, gambler, CEO, ambassador, public relations expert, magistrate, justice of the peace, superintendent, minter of money, customs and excise officer.

Mars

Military man, soldier, policeman, professions related to fire and metal, engineer, chemist, surgeon, dentist, gangster, manufacturer, hangman, guardian, hairdresser, circumciser, carpenter, sculptor, athlete, construction worker, fire-fighter, butcher, machinist, dentist, pharmacist, trainer (sports), soccer player (European football), insurer, glassblower, aircraft engineer, weapons industry, mechanic, general, gunner, bailiff, baker.

Jupiter

Senior manager, minister, politician, ambassador, diplomat, deputy, legal expert, lawyer, judge, tax officer, financier, banker, clergyman, astrologer, philosopher, academician, scholar, doctor, horse trader, horse tamer (and others working with horses), teacher, traveler, travel agent, social worker, sociologist, counselor, international relations or trade expert, gambler, major investor, wholesaler, senator, preacher, investment banker, chancellor, wool draper, entertainer, mentor, diet counselor.

Saturn
Laborers, people who work for a low wage, municipality workers, member of parliament, white-collar employee or civil servant, engineer, contractor, dealer in real estate, miner, industrialist, agricultural engineer, farmer, people who deal with agriculture and farming, gardener, cattleman, people who sell leather, mason, priest, archaeologist, judge, economist, historian, furniture dealers, geologist, organizer, lawmaker, barrister, antiquarian or collector, clown,[1] bricklayer, potter, sexton, shoemaker, dyer, excavator, tanner, horticulturist.

Uranus
Professions related to electricity and electronics, technician, radiologist, car mechanic, television producer, publisher, astrologer, metaphysician, scientist, astronomer, astronaut, electrical and electronics engineer, physician, photographer, mentalist, chemist, mechanical engineer, healer, aircraft workers, metallurgist, antiquarian, sculptor, computer programmer, television and radio worker, airline pilots, film and pop stars, New Age exponents.

Neptune
Diver, submarine worker, sailor, smuggler, psychic, oil field worker, magician, alchemist, irrigation worker, poet, yogi, oracle, astrologer, photographer, mentalist, nurse, chemist, pharmacist, alcohol sellers, fisherman, film industry worker, performer, illustrator, vintner, pop singer, scriptwriter (due to the imagination involved), psychic, confidence trickster, dancer, shoe designer, missionaries, those who work behind the scenes, deep-diver, wine trader.

---

[1] **BD**: Traditionally clowns were sadder characters, and more objects of ridicule than wild comedy characters.

Pluto

Archaeologist, astrobiologist, bacteriologist, alchemist, entomologist, chemist, nuclear physicist, researcher, detective, narcotics expert, investigative judge, miner, geologist, executioner, gravedigger, spy, soothsayer, fortune-teller, astronaut, mafia member, mortician, psychologist, psychiatrist, surgeon, gynecologist, atomic energy expert, healer, insurer, traffic policeman, metaphysician, criminal detective, miner, big businessman.

6: SIGNS AND PROFESSIONS

Here is a compilation of professions by sign, based on attributions found in Julia and Derek Parker, Judith Hall, Rex E. Bills, and my own contributions.

Aries
Fireman, soldier, military men, army officer, athletes, business owner, self-employment, publicity agent, team sports instructor, policeman, doctor, surgeon, inspector, party leader, team leader, metallurgist, physical therapist, satirist, entrepreneur, racing driver, electrician, herbalist, naturopath, actor, showman, creative works, occupations connected with fire and/or metal, service station owners, someone who works with sharp and edged tools.

Taurus
Musician, singer, dancer, artisan, art dealer, sculptor, body artist, jeweler, cosmetologist, soap maker, restaurant owner, restauranteur, cook, chef, beautician, luxury trader, real estate agent, gardener, farmer, confectioner, designer, florist, architect, gourmet, cabinet maker, geologist, soft furnishings industry, wine trade, fashion industry, welfare work, leather worker, craft worker.

Gemini
Journalist, writer, teacher, researcher, investigator, lecturer, editor, merchant, salesman, trade exhibition consultant, secretary, driver, traffic manager, train conductor, receptionist, analyst, barrister, foreign correspondent, publisher, book seller, bookkeeper, librarian, linguist, librarian, mail carrier, messenger, broadcasting technician, broadcaster, computer operator, engineer, nerve specialist, telephone repairman/operator/salesman, travel agent or guide, advertiser, demonstrator, communication industry, the me-

dia, press, telecommunications, departments of buying and selling, market management, travel industry, public relations, carpentry, airlines, transportation industry, commentating.

Cancer

Swimming instructor or swimmer, sailor, caterer, dairy farmer, nurse, nanny, pharmacist, chef, cook, baker, restaurant owner, kindergarten teacher, hotel manager, hotelier, real estate agent, historian, antiquarian, shipping agent, dietician, welfare officer, midwife, gynecologist, therapist, fishmonger, physical therapist, agriculturist, hotel keeper and worker, taproom owner, tavern owner, human resources director, housing officer, the navy, hotel business, grocery trades, fishing industry, diving, ship building and design, charity field work, ecology, child care, house decorating business, social worker, care worker.

Leo

Prime minister, President, governor, manager, chairmen, director, organizer, politician, sportsmen, dancer, designer, artist, actor, film star, model, performer, theater manager, art teacher, lighting specialist, display artist, production team leader, jewelry trader, businessman, manager, entertainer, chief, head-waiter, harbor master, broker, forester, gambler, goldsmith, speculator, supervisor, stock exchanger, TV producer or presenter, fashion designer, heating engineer, cardiologist, cardiac surgeon, creative works, jewelry or fine art trades, big business, game industry, gambling, professions connected with play and leisure.

Virgo

Literary agent, analyst, researcher, accountant, financial consultant, mathematician, organic farmer, editor, literary critic, writer, teacher, lecturer, journalist, printer, librarian, craft worker, craftsman, dispatch rider, builder, graphologist, sales assistant, scientist, doctor, homeopath, medical researcher, pharmacist, hygienist, nutritionist, nurse, chemist, microbiologist, horticulture, biologist, veterinarian, dietician, restorer, tailor, copywriter, computer programmer, locksmith, ecologist, domestic servant, waiter, restaurant proprietor, secretary, statistician, data processor, linguist, the working class in general, the stationery trade.

Libra
Artisan, beautician, hairdresser, fashion designer, painter, decorator, model, actor or actress, confectioner, dressmaker, tailor, furniture salesperson, restorer, diplomat, librarian, bookseller, cosmetologist, florist, juggler, lawyer, judge, wigmaker, graphic artist, image consultant, art dealer, therapist, the fashion industry, luxury trades, the dress rental business, customer relations, public relations, drapery trades, jewelry trades, furnishing, confectionary, negotiators, conciliators, consultants.

Scorpio
Psychologist, psychiatrist, doctor, surgical operator, dentist, engineer, metallurgist, police, soldier, detective, inspector, executioner, pathologist, criminal expert, genealogist, gynecologist, surgeon, solicitor, biologist, car repairer, TV engineer, barber, butcher, chemist, tax collector, junk dealer, magician, surveillance operator, hypnotherapist, sex therapist, submariner, diver, mining, the marines, the vine trade, banking, insurance, detective work, narcotics, criminal investigation, private investigation, medical profession, apothecaries, pharmacists, chemical laboratories, undertakers, nuclear weapons, sewage worker.

Sagittarius
Instructor, teacher, lecturer, publisher, professor, researcher, writer, churchmen, clergymen, lawyer, judge, translator, explorer, expedition organizer, news agent, travel agent, sportsmen, sports

trainer, bookseller, anthropologist, riding instructor, linguist, zoologist, geographer, tour operator, pilot, hostess, international relations specialist, advertising agent, radio or television announcer, interpreter, croupier, the travel industry, advertising, the import-export business, literary work, universities, publishing, advisors, consultants, the internet, map-making, airlines, international tradesmen, foreign affairs and trade, publicity directors, sporting goods and equipment dealers, public relations consultant.

Capricorn

Prime minister, governor, officer, forester, economist, broker, insurance specialist, real estate agent, land dealer, mining engineer, architect, farmer, mason, scientific researcher, archaeologist, geologist, metallurgist, mathematician, anthropologist, brick maker, builder, carpenter, cemetery worker, efficiency expert, jailor, organizer, sculptor, law enforcement officer, orthopedic surgeon, osteopath, dentist, surveyor, bureaucrats, CEOs, civil servants, stock exchange, insurance, the economy in general, local government, mining, landscape gardening, plumbing, town planning, mountaineer, inventor, businessmen, building trades, welfare work.

Aquarius

Scientist, space researcher, astronaut, astronomer, astrologer, meteorologist, electrical engineer, computer programmer, radiographer, radiologist, wireless operator, glazier, radio and TV reporter-announcer, hydrographer, chemist, curator, psychotherapist, innovator, automobile manufacturer or dealer, parliamentarian, technician, quantum physicist, systems analyst, electrical engineer, ecological consultant, futures trader, cognitive therapist, archaeologist, the air force, airlines, pilots, ecological research, space industry, humanitarian works, orthopedic medicine, television, technologies, professions related to electricity and electronics, creative and scientific works, New Age professions.

Pisces

Artist, poet, musician, dancer, movie star, scriptwriter, filmmaker, film editor, cameraman, photographer, illustrator, artisan, designer, fantasy or occult writer, shoe trader, reflexologist, social worker, horticulture, psychotherapist, homeopath, spiritualist, diver, monk, sailor, seaman, shipper, hypnotherapist, healer, tarot reader, podiatrist, fishmonger, the navy, audio/visual trades, fashion design, works near the sea, charity works, the caring professions, cinema, drama, lingerie trades, prison service, mining (oil), creative craft work, the priesthood, shoe sales, gasoline stations, hospital workers, jailors, spirit mediums, spies, alcohol counselor.

7: PLANETS LOCATED IN THE 10th HOUSE

Planets located in the 10th house indicate not only the fields in which the native may be successful, but also how and to what extent he will achieve success.

The Moon in the 10th house
This position may bring the support of top management and authority figures, especially female ones. The native's mother may influence the native's decisions concerning his personal development, career, and other important decisions in life. The native may choose a profession which gives emotional satisfaction and meets the needs of society. Professions related to women are more suitable.

Mercury in the 10th house
This position may bring success through good communication with top management and authority figures. It is beneficial for professions in trade, writing, teaching, and mathematics. Professions that require mental activities are prominent. Success comes through careful planning and strategic thinking. It represent a tendency for private sector work, academic studies, writing, journalism, politics, and the communication industry.

Venus in the 10th house
This position brings the support of authority figures. There is a strong possibility of success in social and artistic fields. Partnerships also bring success. Good relations with higher-ups are prominent. This is an ideal alignment for being involved in the arts.

The Sun in the 10th house

This position brings recognition, fame, and the support of authority figures. The native may be an executive manager or he may be his own brand. He may be working at the top management level. If the Sun is dignified and not afflicted, the native may build up a reputation throughout his whole life.

Mars in the 10th house

This position brings difficulties in getting the support of authority figures. The native may need to struggle, make effort, and fight for success in his career. It indicates competition and conflicts. The ambition for gaining a reputation in the career and showing it off is high.

Jupiter in the 10th house

This position enables getting the support of authority figures. It brings big chances for being successful in the career. It indicates recognition and coming to important positions. The native may work in managerial positions, may be an ambassador or diplomat (which are honorable professions). It also brings success in finance, education, and juridical fields.

Saturn in the 10th house

The native with this position in his chart may have difficulties in getting the support of people in authoritative positions. It may bring experience in professional issues, he may be faced with restrictions and delay, but he may reach success in the long term, even if he needs to pay the price for success. This position may indicate that professional success is important for the native and he is ambitious in career matters.

Uranus in the 10th house

Unexpected developments related to career and profession, ups and downs, sudden detachments, quitting one's job, and changing jobs often, may be seen. The native displays radical attitudes in professional issues. He may be prone to professions related to computers, electronics, aviation, and other extraordinary fields. He may find recognition in his career by combining his originality with creativity.

Neptune in the 10th house

It may bring success in professional fields where the native may use his imagination and creativity. The film industry, advertising, music, and fashion are among these fields. Charitable works, service and improvement operations, and professions related to water, the sea, oil, and chemicals may be suitable. The native who has this position should be careful with regard to fraud and scandals.

Pluto in the 10th house

It may bring self-realization through challenges and a passion for power and recognition. The native may be successful in authoritative positions. He should be careful not to display dictatorial tendencies. He may experience destruction and restoration in profession matters.

8: SIGNS ON THE CUSP OF THE 10TH

Aries on the cusp of the 10th house:
The native desires to be successful through his own efforts and motivation; he fights for his desires and acts courageously and passionately to realize his goals. He is ambitious and outgoing. He wants to reveal his leadership talents. He has difficulties when others remain in the forefront, and does not want to be dominated by others. In such an environment, he might either fight and seize the leadership, or quit. He may be successful in professions that require research. He is innovative, a pioneer, competitive, and fearless. If he owns a business, or if he is the manager, he does not avoid risks and acts as a leader, directly and energetically. His greatest risk is his restlessness, acting without thinking, and an inability to stop being aggressive. He has difficulties in professions that require partnerships and cooperation.

Taurus on the cusp of the 10th house:
The native needs security in his professional field. He may gain firm ground in time through his efforts. He probably performs his profession for many years. His first rule in business life is to maintain concrete results. He does not feel comfortable in professions which are based on fantasies and imagination. He has a great need for security in business life. He prefers professions which bring him regular income. He does not have difficulties in taking responsibility. As a manager or boss, he values loyalty and cares about his employees' security. He is talented in earning money as a business man. However, he avoids big risks. For him, the best investment is one which offers him security and continuity. He works ambitiously no matter what the working conditions are. He has certain rules and is strict in them. He may be very successful in the banking sec-

tor, monetary markets, and the fields like home decoration, fashion and beauty, luxury goods, arts, real estate, and gardening.

Gemini on the cusp of the 10th house:
The native's success depends on his flexible, harmonious, and multi-dimensional personality. He may be busy with many different things simultaneously and prefer a profession which provides the variety he requires and also satisfies his mental needs. His curiosity and eagerness to learn is also seen in his professional life. He always goes after new information and developments. He may be a good researcher, journalist, author, or academician. He may make quick decisions about his business and future plans, and change his decisions frequently. He may be involved in two different jobs at the same time. Dealing with a single thing may be boring and inadequate for him. He runs the risk of being scattered. Instead of working at a fixed place, he may prefer professions that offer a change of settings. As a manager or employer, he is talented at problem solving. He prefers acting flexibly according to changing conditions, so his decisions may change. He respects smart and new ideas, and is flexible in his decisions.

Cancer on the cusp of the 10th house:
The native does everything to protect his reputation. He may work in industries like real estate, dining, lodging, and natural therapies, he may be a nurse or deal with trade or the family business. He is also successful in decoration, design, and the fashion industry. He cannot remain in an atmosphere where he does not feel emotionally secure. He is emotionally attached to his job and his colleagues, which is why he may try to make his working environment feel like a family environment. He feels attached to the people he works with and does not leave them alone. He may undertake his friends' duties to help them. He may sometimes get a reaction due to his over-emotional attitudes and caprice. If he is

well motivated, he works willingly and does a good job. As an employer, he is very empathetic. He tries to help his employees. His biggest disadvantage is that he reflects his emotions into his works and has emotional reactions.

Leo on the cusp of the 10ᵗʰ house:
The native may struggle to achieve a respectful and competent position in his career. He has the potential to take responsibility and to organize others. He trusts himself and his talents fully. He wants to stand somewhere in his career where he can earn others' respect. His honor and dignity is more important than money. He likes being in contact with powerful people. He is ambitious. It is hard for him to change his mind. When he is a manager or employer, he will reveal his absolute power. He does everything to finish his work, he does not abort the things he started. Managerial positions are suitable. He wants to be the manager of the field he is in. He likes taking risks. He is always at the center and others should be around him. He likes presenting himself to society and he wants to be recognized.

Virgo on the cusp of the 10ᵗʰ house:
The native attaches importance to professional matters. For him, business life is very serious; he makes his decisions through careful analysis. He has the ability to work carefully and meticulously. Due to his sharp wit and practicality, he may work in the service sector, office environment, health sector, computer and research fields, and academic fields. He may be an excellent accountant. He may be successful in professions related to health and hygiene. As a manager or employer, he cannot tolerate untidiness. He wants others to obey general rules. As he does not like risks, he avoids ventures which seem ambiguous. He does not need to be in the forefront. He is successful in the service sector. He should earn money in order to feel secure.

Libra on the cusp of the 10ᵗʰ house:

The native may take advantage of his sociable, diplomatic, and polite attitudes. He may cooperate well with others and benefit from partnerships. Professions which let him communicate with others are suitable. He is talented at professions connected with mediation, cooperative activities, representing others, and consultations. He brings balance and harmony to business life and does not work at any place where there is no peace. He prefers earning less money in a comfortable environment, than earning more money under severe conditions. His understanding of justice and equality is highly developed and he is talented at generating consensus. He may work in the legal and political arena. He likes getting the opinions of his employees and evaluates those opinions. He is fair in sharing rights. He does not like risky businesses. He may be successful at professions which suit his sense of aesthetics. He may be an architect or work in decoration and the fashion industry. As a manager or employer, indecisiveness is his greatest disadvantage.

Scorpio on the cusp of the 10ᵗʰ house:

The native may reach his personal goals and desires through effort and hard work (both mental and physical). He is talented at research. He is enduring: he either takes responsibility for his duties and completes them, or does not them at all. His strong intuitions are the key to his success. He is a deep investigator, researcher, and uncoverer of things. He knows all of the strengths and weaknesses of his business competitors: that's why everyone may shrink from or avoid him. He likes competition and wants to beat his competitors. He is emotional, but does not reveal his emotions in business life. As an employer he may appear cruel. He may eliminate employees when needed. As an employee, he may be very successful due to his stubborn, decisive, and ambitious nature. He likes dangerous and risky professions. So, he may be a successful policeman, soldier, or detective. He may also be successful in fields like medicine, human anatomy, and psychology.

Sagittarius on the cusp of the 10th house:

The native earns the respect of others through teaching and revealing his wisdom. He may be suitable for professions related to law, education, travel, publishing, and even theology. He is an optimist, idealist, and dedicated to his aims in matters related to his career. He pushes the limits and does not know how to say no. As an employer he does not like desk jobs: he prefers professions where he can be mobile. He is talented in tourism and foreign trade. He may need to improve himself: for example, he may want to learn foreign languages in order to be successful in his profession or to expand his social circle. He may easily take risks. He does not like a boring business life. He should be free in his career.

Capricorn on the cusp of the 10th house:

The native's profession may be the most important subject of his life. He prefers taking sound and lasting steps instead of making quick progress. He is disciplined and organized while working; he makes long-term plans and proceeds slowly but surely. He is highly ambitious and success-oriented. Although he may sometimes have difficulties in believing in himself, he may easily overcome all obstacles when he is focused on success. His sense of duty and discipline is really advanced. He is a man of the system, either as an employer or employee. He is aware of the ruthless aspects of business life. He is motivated by the respect of others and the self-reliance he feels after his achievements. He is an ideal manager. He applies the rules and make others adhere to them successfully. He does not attempt things which are not approved of by society. He does not like taking big risks. He is very cautious. He feels uncomfortable with ups and downs. He likes routine in business life, and monotony does not make him feel uncomfortable. He may devote himself to his career. He may be successful in professions which require detailed research and execution, in governmental or organizational affairs, or engineering.

Aquarius on the cusp of the 10th house:

The native may tend towards the fields which have contemporary and progressive features. He closely follows developments related to his profession. He is interested in extraordinary professions and with technology, sociology, systems analysis, and aviation. He may be successful in professions that require mental activities he could use in his creativity. He is in pursuit of professions which are different and ahead of their time, visionary. Professions which are popular in our century are suitable for him. He may easily reveal his talents and creativity in professions related to astrology, alternative medicine, the internet, electronics, and music. If he cannot realize his own distinctive approach in conventional professions and bring innovation, he may quit. As an employer he expects an independent environment. If supported, he may show progress due to his inventive and innovative style. As a manager or employer, he respects human rights. He is egalitarian and respects alternatives in management. He takes risks in different issues which have no alternative. He may devote his whole life to such an issue.

Pisces on the cusp of the 10th house:

The native may be involved in professions which are universal and where he may sacrifice himself. He may strive to understand life's spiritual aspects and work in fields where he can contribute to the spiritual development of others. He has the potential to be involved in artistic activities which require creativity. He has a huge imagination. He is talented in the arts. His success depends on his ability to see the whole picture and having a vision. He is not good at details. He may make mistakes as he gets scattered quickly and cannot easily focus. He does not like risks and speculations. His greatest disadvantages are making decisions based on his emotions and indecisiveness. He may change jobs frequently. He is not stubborn and enduring. As an employee he may be scattered quickly as he is over-sensitive, and he may be cast down easily. As he has a transcendent imagination, desk jobs and routines may hamper his talents. He is interested and talented in mysticism.

Additionally, based on the quadruplicities, if one of the cardinal signs is on the cusp of the 10th house, the native may be prone to changing jobs frequently. If it is a fixed sign, the native tends to do the same job for a long time. If a mutable sign, the native may be exposed to job changes and can do two jobs simultaneously.

9: THE LORD OF THE 10TH IN THE HOUSES

The lord of the 10th in the 1st:

The native's success and achievements in life stem from his own efforts and ventures. He may be his own boss or may at least impose his working conditions on others. This is one of the positions that can really bring professional success. The native may achieve success without too much effort. The people in influential and important positions may support the native and be on his side.

The lord of the 10th in the 2nd:

The native earns his living through his own career or profession. If he works for others, he wants to earn a salary which fits his status and reputation. This position brings profit due to the career. The native's profession may be something like trade, which directly brings him money. Through earning money due to business, the native's confidence increases and he attaches importance in earning money from his career.

The lord of the 10th in the 3rd:

The native's reputation may be a result of his communication skills, like speaking and writing. As long as he has authority in his profession, he may be easily listened to by others. If the significator is in one of the cadent houses, then it may take time or require more effort to show himself. Siblings, his inner circle, and travel may be an important part of his business. The native may work in fields like education, publishing, media, telecommunications, communications, or transportation; he may express himself through writing or speaking.

The lord of the 10th in the 4th:

The native's home and career lives may be closely related to each other. He may take work home, or have home-related work. His family may be influential in his career. He may work from home, or make a family business. He may work in the real estate sector. In any case, the lord of the career house is located in a strong house, and this increases the chance for professional success. Success may come in native's later years.

The lord of the 10th in the 5th:

The native's profession may be related to the arts, the entertainment sector, sports, fashion, or the hospitality industry. It brings the chance of enjoying work, or a profession including some entertainment in it. The native's hobby may turn into a profession. He may be involved in professions related to children or young people. If the lord of the 10th is in a favorable house, the native may be successful in his career.

The lord of the 10th in the 6th:

The native's approach to working may be reflected in his professional prestige. He may get recognition and respect as long as he becomes an expert in a specific field. He may get recognition through much effort; he needs to work hard. Sometimes he may feel anxious about success and this may lead to underperformance. His success depends on his team. His profession may be related to health and healing, or the service sector.

The lord of the 10th in the 7th:

The native's career will probably lead him to get in touch with the people directly and to make professional partnerships. He may be a consultant who is in contact with people on a one-to-one basis. He may also be a lawyer, doctor, psychologist, or astrologer, in close touch with his clients. He may find success easily if the lord of the 10ᵗʰ house is favorably located.

The lord of the 10ᵗʰ in the 8ᵗʰ:
The native's profession may be related to other people's money: the banking, finance, and insurance sectors. The native may earn profit from partnerships. In case of things going wrong in business, he may feel anxious. He may have to get over some crises and difficulties.

The lord of the 10ᵗʰ in the 9ᵗʰ:
Travel may be an important element of the native's profession. The native may potentially be involved in academic studies, publishing, law, consulting, or in professions related to religion. Astrology and some scientific matters may also attract the native. In any case, the native wants to expand to the world and reach great masses of people. The native's profession also expands his vision and life view.

The lord of the 10ᵗʰ in the 10ᵗʰ:
The native wants to earn a reputation in his career and show it to the whole world. He may be an authority in a certain field, or a celebrity. He may work in his own business. He may be supported by people in authority. This is one of the strongest placements in terms of achieving professional success and displaying it. If the lord of the 10ᵗʰ house is a benefic or supported by a benefic, the chance for success increases.

The lord of the 10ᵗʰ in the 11ᵗʰ:
The people in the native's social groups and his friends may be charitable, and they may contribute to his professional success. The native's profession may be related to clubs, organizations, charities, and parties where masses of people are involved. This

position brings the native opportunity and profit through his profession. His profession helps the native expand his social circle.

The lord of the 10th in the 12th:

The native may have difficulties gaining professional recognition. He does not like taking center stage; he prefers working behind the scenes. This is one of the most difficult places for achieving professional success. He may be overthrown due to hidden enemies and behind-the-scenes activities. If the significator is in a favorable position, the native may be working in isolation; perhaps he may be an author, or he may be involved in the healing industry and be a doctor, nurse, or psychologist.

Appendix A: Table of Dignities

		♈	♉	♊	♋	♌	♍	♎	♏	♐	♑	♒	♓	
ESSENTIAL DEBILITIES	FALL	♄		☋	♂		♀	☉	☽	☊	♃		☿	(-4)
	DETRIMENT	♀	♂	♃	♄	♄	♃	♂	♀	☿	☽	☉	☿	(-5)
		♈	♉	♊	♋	♌	♍	♎	♏	♐	♑	♒	♓	
ESSENTIAL DIGNITIES: DOMICILE RULERSHIP		♂	♀	☿	☽	☉	☿	♀	♂	♃	♄	♄	♃	(+5)
EXALTATION		☉	☽	☊	♃		☿	♄		☋	♂		♀	(+4)
		19	3	3	15		15	21		3	28		27	
TRIPLICITY RULERS *Trigon Lords (Dorotheus)*	DAY	☉	♀	♄	♀	☉	♀	♄	♀	☉	♀	♄	♀	(+3)
	NIGHT	♃	☽	☿	♂	♃	☽	☿	♂	♃	☽	☿	♂	
	COMMON	♄	♂	♃	☽	♄	♂	♃	☽	♄	♂	♃	☽	
TERMS *Bounds (Egyptian)*		♃ (0° - 5° 59')	♀ (0° - 7° 59')	☿ (0° - 5° 59')	♂ (0° - 6° 59')	♃ (0° - 5° 59')	☿ (0° - 6° 59')	♄ (0° - 5° 59')	♂ (0° - 6° 59')	♃ (0° - 11° 59')	☿ (0° - 6° 59')	☿ (0° - 6° 59')	♀ (0° - 11° 59')	(+2)
		♀ (6° - 11° 59')	☿ (8° - 13° 59')	♃ (6° - 11° 59')	♀ (7° - 12° 59')	♀ (6° - 10° 59')	♀ (7° - 16° 59')	☿ (6° - 13° 59')	♀ (7° - 10° 59')	♀ (12° - 16° 59')	♃ (7° - 13° 59')	♀ (7° - 12° 59')	♃ (12° - 15° 59')	
		☿ (12° - 19° 59')	♃ (14° - 21° 59')	♀ (12° - 16° 59')	☿ (13° - 18° 59')	♄ (11° - 17° 59')	♃ (17° - 20° 59')	♃ (14° - 20° 59')	☿ (11° - 18° 59')	☿ (17° - 20° 59')	♀ (14° - 21° 59')	♃ (13° - 19° 59')	☿ (16° - 18° 59')	
		♂ (20° - 24° 59')	♄ (22° - 26° 59')	♂ (17° - 23° 59')	♃ (19° - 25° 59')	☿ (18° - 23° 59')	♂ (21° - 27° 59')	♀ (21° - 27° 59')	♃ (19° - 23° 59')	♄ (21° - 25° 59')	♄ (22° - 25° 59')	♂ (20° - 24° 59')	♂ (19° - 27° 59')	
		♄ (25° - 29° 59')	♂ (27° - 29° 59')	♄ (24° - 29° 59')	♄ (26° - 29° 59')	♂ (24° - 29° 59')	♄ (28° - 29° 59')	♂ (28° - 29° 59')	♄ (24° - 29° 59')	♂ (26° - 29° 59')	♂ (26° - 29° 59')	♄ (25° - 29° 59')	♄ (28° - 29° 59')	
DECANIC FACES *(Chaldean)*	1. DECAN (00° 00' - 9° 59')	♂	☿	♃	♀	♄	☉	☽	♂	☿	♃	♀	♄	(+1)
	2. DECAN (10° 00' - 19° 59')	☉	☽	♂	☿	♃	♀	♄	☉	☽	♂	☿	♃	
	3. DECAN (20° 00' - 29° 59')	♀	♄	☉	☽	♂	☿	♃	♀	♄	☉	☽	♂	

Appendix B: How to Calculate Victors

In traditional astrology, there are two ways of calculating a victor. One of them is to calculate the victor over a single zodiacal degree or significator in the chart. The other is to find out the victor over several degrees or significators.

The reason for calculating the victor over a single point is to find the most authoritative planet over that zodiacal degree. In other words, wherever a single significator (such as a planet or Lot) is located the victor over that degree is the planet which is the most influential over that significator. For any degree, the domicile or sign lord gets 5 points, the exalted lord 4, the triplicity lord 3, the term lord 2, and face ruler 1.

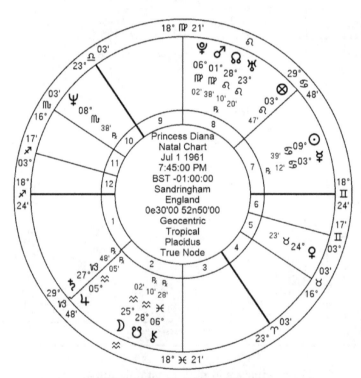

Figure 24: Princess Diana

The reason for finding a composite victor over several places is a little bit different: when some topic has several significators at once, the victor over all of them together is the planet which has the most to say about that subject. So if we are studying on marriage, we should calculate the victor over the following places: the degree of the 7th house cusp, the degree of its lord, any planet in the 7th, the Lot of marriage, the lord of the Lot, and Venus: we can do these one at a time and add up the scores for each ruler at the end, or do them all at once in a single, large table. The planet with the highest score is the victor and will have the most to say about the issues related to marriage.

Let's practice how to calculate victors using Princess Diana's chart, starting with the victor over her Ascendant (18° 24' Sagittarius). First, with the help of the table of dignities (Appendix A), the lord of the sign (Jupiter) gets 5 points. There is no exalted lord of Sagittarius, so no planet gets 4 points. Sagittarius is a fiery sign, and those signs have the Sun, Jupiter, and Saturn as their triplicity lords: each of them gets 3 points. The term ruler of the Ascendant is Mercury, who gets 2 points. The face lord is the Moon, who gets 1 point:

Jupiter: 5 + 3 = 8
Sun: 3
Saturn: 3
Mercury: 2
Moon: 1

Jupiter has the highest score, so the victor over the degree of her Ascendant is Jupiter.

The composite victor uses the same method, but we need to calculate the victor over several degrees at once. Count up the points for the lords of each place separately, then then add up the totals: the planet with the highest score is the composite victor.

Appendix C: How to Find the Victor of the Chart

The victor of the chart is the key of the chart and the native's life; it represents the force that dominates the native's life. It may also be considered as describing the native's primary characteristics. To find victor of a chart, follow the steps below:

1. Prepare a table in which you record which planets have rulerships over the following places: the degrees of the Sun, Moon, Ascendant, Lot of Fortune, and the SAN (the pre-natal New or Full Moon) before birth. The domicile or sign lord of each of these places gets 5 points, the exalted lord 4, the triplicity lords 3, the term lord 2, and face ruler 1.

2. Give each of the seven traditional planets points based on which house it is in:

House	1	10	7	4	11	5	2	9	8	3	12	6
Points	12	11	10	9	8	7	6	5	4	3	2	1

For example, if the Sun is in the 3rd house, he gets 3 points.

3. Assign 7 points to the ruler of the day on which the native was born.

4. Assign 6 points to the ruler of the hour in which the native was born.

Add up the points for each planet: the planet with the highest score is the victor of the chart.

Appendix D: How to Calculate Lots

Lots (formerly called "Arabic Parts") are chart positions which signify certain topics, and are derived from the positions of three other things (often, two planets and the Ascendant). In the older texts, the Lots were calculated by counting the degrees from the first position or planet, forward in the zodiac to the second one, and then projecting that same number of degrees and minutes from the third point (usually the Ascendant): where the counting stops, is the position of the Lot. The counting between the first two points was usually reversed for nocturnal charts. For example, the diurnal calculation for the Lot of Fortune is: from the Sun forward to the Moon, and project from the Ascendant. But by night, one counts from the Moon forward to the Sun, and projects from the Ascendant. (In some modern astrology texts, there is no reversal by night.)

To make the calculations precise, it is useful to convert the degrees of the three positions into absolute longitude (between 0° and 360°), and add and subtract those values. For example, let's assume we have a chart in which the Moon is at 28° 28' Scorpio, the Sun at 23° 36' Aquarius, and the Ascendant 1° 15' Libra. Now, let's calculate the Lot of Fortune using these three reference points:

Diurnal: ASC + Moon – Sun
Nocturnal: ASC + Sun – Moon

Since the chart is nocturnal, we use the nocturnal formula. But first we must convert the longitudes of the luminaries and the Ascendant to absolute longitudes by adding the degrees of the beginning of their signs, then perform the calculation, and finally convert the result back into zodiacal degrees:

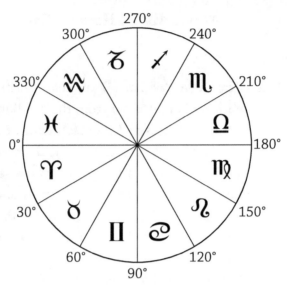

For example, the Ascendant is at 1° 15' Libra, which is 1° 15' more than the beginning of Libra (180°): so after adding the 180°, can say the Ascendant is at 181° 15'. (We can add 360° to eliminate sums that are negative, or subtract it for those over 360°).

ASC: 181° 15'
+ Sun: 323° 36'
<u>- Moon: 238° 28'</u>
266° 23' = **26° 23' Sagittarius**

See my chart in Figure 4 to verify this result.

Appendix E: Glossary

Accidental Benefic: A malefic planet located in one of the benefic houses; in dignity and not afflicted; bringing limited benefit but no affliction at all.

Accidental Dignity: The strength a planet gains for some reason other than its zodiacal position. Planets located in the angular houses fulfill 100% of their promises; planets located in the succeedent houses fulfill 50% of their promises, and planets in the cadent houses fulfill 25% of their promises.

Accidental Malefic: A benefic planet located in one of the malefic houses; in detriment, fall or afflicted; bringing affliction more than benefits.

Afflicted; Impeded: An indicator of weakness. It means being restricted, disabled and ill. Afflicted planets cannot fulfill their promises. States that afflict the planets are described in detail in Bonatti's *146 Considerations*. The most important afflictions are being located in cadent houses, being burned, retrograde, and being in conjunction, square, or opposition with malefics without reception.

Alcocoden: See **House-master**.

Alien: A planet having no essential dignities. Often called "peregrine." Such a planet is similar to a foreigner who travels in a foreign country and who has no rights or no business there. Its state in this position is linked with the ruler of this place.

Almutem Figuris: See **Victor of the chart**.

Almuten: See **Victor**.

Analogy: The similarity/ parallelism of the nature of the planets with the houses and signs they are in.

Anaretic: Derived from Greek; refers to a point that is fatal and destroying in primary directions.

Angles: The main structural keys of the chart, which give the primary house themes and planetary strength. Planets located in the angular houses have stronger and more visible impacts.

Angular Houses: see **Cardinal Houses.**

Aphelion: The point in the orbit of a planet where it is farthest from the Sun.

Aphetic: Refers to places which are suitable for the longevity **releaser** or "hyleg" to be in.

Arabic Parts: See **Lots.**

Ascendant: The degree of the zodiac which crosses the eastern horizon, and in quadrant house systems the cusp of the 1st house. The sign to which this degree belongs, is the "rising sign."

Aspects: From words that mean "to look at," configurations between two places in the zodiac which give information about how planets especially express their influences. on how the planets express their influences. The six "Ptolemaic" aspects are at intervals of 60°, 90°, 120°, and 180°. The conjunction is usually included among these, although it is not an aspect.

Bad Houses: 6th, 8th, and 12th houses.

Bad Placement: Being placed in its detriment or fall, being cadent, or being in a conjunction or aspect with malefics.

Badly Disposed: Being placed in a weak house and being not dignified. Having incompatible aspects and no contact with its ruler also makes a planet badly disposed.

Being in dignity: A planet which has at least one of the major dignities (domicile, exaltation, triplicity, term and face rulerships) is in dignity. The most powerful dignities are domicile and exaltation rulerships.

Benefics, Benefic Planets: Benefics are planets that assist the native in a positive outcome without making too much effort, bring benefits, support, and balance him in a moderate way. Benefic planets are Jupiter, Venus and the Sun. The waxing Moon and in some cases Mercury may also be considered benefics.

Besieged, Enclosure: A planet which lies between two planets (especially the malefics). A planet may be besieged through a conjunction or an aspect.

Burned: A planet which is 8.5° close to the Sun. A burned planet is afflicted. It is one of the debilities. According to ancient astrologers, it is the most serious debility.

Cadent Houses: 3rd, 6th, 9th, and 12th houses.

Cardinal Houses: 1st, 4th, 7th, and 10th houses. Also known as angular houses.

Cazimi: When a planet is within the 17' of the Sun, it is cazimi. A cazimi planet is "in the heart of the Sun" and so it is under some kind of divine protection as it is so close to the Sun's spirit.

Combust: See **Burned.**

Debility, debilitated: A planet located in the sign of its detriment or fall, where a planet is in the sign opposite the sign it rules (detriment) or is exalted (fall). Such planets cannot fulfill their promises. Malefics so debilitated cause trouble, so their malefic impacts increase. According to some astrologers, being placed in a weak house, having hard aspects with the malefics, being retrograde, and being burned are also debilities.

Declination: The angular distance of a planet north or south of the celestial equator.

Derived Houses: Houses counted from other places or houses, in order to see the chart from a broader perspective. For example, the 2nd natal house indicates the native's money; but because the 5th house is the 2nd from the 4th (indicating the father), the 5th house also indicates the father's money in addition to its normal signification for children.

Dignity: The strength, advantage, or virtue of a planet. This word is also used to describe the various types of rulerships a planet has.

Dispositor: A planet which rules the sign that another planet is located in. For example, if Venus is in Aries, she is disposed by Mars.

Diurnal Planets: Sun, Jupiter, and Saturn.

Domicile Rulership: If a planet is placed in a house that it rules, it feels as if it is at its own home. It displays its nature comfortably and fulfills its promises. For example, the Moon is the domicile ruler of Cancer.

Double-Bodied Signs: The mutable signs, which are Gemini, Virgo, Sagittarius, and Pisces.

Descendant: The point opposite the **Ascendant**, where the zodiac crosses the western horizon.

Duodecimae: See **Twelfth-parts.**

Eastern: Planets which rise before the Sun. Planets which are eastern of the Sun are powerful; they may fulfill their promises efficiently; acceptable and praiseworthy. According to the rules of medieval astrology, Mercury and Venus are eastern when they rise after the Sun.

Eastern Quarters: The quarters of the chart between the ASC-MC and DSC-IC.

Ecliptic: The plane defined by the Sun's motion, which the zodiac is centered on.

Electional Astrology: The branch of astrology used for choosing the right time for actions, often consulted for business ventures, surgical operations, signing agreements, buying and selling, etc.

Elevation; Elevated: A planet which is close to the Midheaven, even if having passed more than 5° beyond it. This placement indicates the things that the native prioritizes.

Essential Dignity: A dignity which a planet has through the zodiac (such as being in the sign of its exaltation). A planet located in one of these dignities have the power to fulfill its promises, but domicile and exaltation rulership are strongest.

Exaltation Rulership: A planet in its own exaltation is like a person who is near the king, who is respected and rewarded. Having exaltation rulership lets the nature of the planet be manifested plainly. For example: the Sun is the exalted ruler of Aries, and when in it he is "exalted."

Face: Each 10° of the zodiac: each sign has three faces, with 36 total in the zodiac. Each face is ruled by a planet: for example, the second face lord of Gemini is Mars. Although face rulership brings the least dignity, it is important anyway.

Feminine Planets: Moon, Venus, and sometimes Mercury

Final Dispositor: A final dispositor is a planet which all other planets are ultimately dependent on because it is the only one in its own sign of the zodiac (like the Sun in Leo).

Fixed Stars: Fixed stars for the constellations. Unlike the planets, fixed stars look stationary from the earth; but due to the precession of the equinoxes they move less than 1' per year and 1° every 72 years. Those closest to the ecliptic, and the brightest, have distinguished importance.

Friendly Planets: Planets which are compatible with each other, having the same natures.

Good Houses: Houses except the 6th, 12th, and 8th houses.

Good Placement: Being placed in its dignity or in strong houses, well-aspected and contact with its ruler.

Halb: One of the minor dignities indicating that a planet will be more active and influential. In a diurnal chart, if a diurnal planet is above the horizon (or in a nocturnal chart below the horizon), then it is *halb*. In a nocturnal chart, if a nocturnal planet is above the horizon (or in a diurnal chart below the horizon(, then it is *halb*.

Hayz: From the Arabic word *hayyiz* which means "domain": a minor dignity which is more influential than *halb*. In a diurnal chart, if a diurnal planet is above the horizon (or in a nocturnal chart below the horizon) and in one of the masculine signs, then it is in its *hayz* or domain. Similarly, in a nocturnal chart if a nocturnal planet is above the horizon (or in a diurnal chart below the horizon) and in one of the feminine signs, then it is in its *hayz* or domain.

Horary Astrology: A branch of astrology dealing with questions "of the hour." The astrologer erects the chart for the moment he understands the client's question, and makes a prediction. Horary astrology was widely used because people often did not know their exact birth time.

Hostile Planets: Planets which are incompatible with each other, having opposite natures.

House-master: Derived from a Persian word indicating a planet that grants years in longevity techniques.

Houses: The division of a chart into 12 sections, each of which signifies a particular realm of experience or life. The houses where the planets are located in a chart are important factors in reading.

Hyleg: See **Releaser**.

IC (Imum Coeli): The part of the zodiac passing the lower meridian to the north, and in quadrant houses the cusp of the 4th house. It is opposite the **MC**.

In contact: In aspect or conjunction with something.

Increasing in Light: The process by which the Moon's light increases until it is full.

Intercepted Sign: A sign which has no cusp on it.

Joys: Planets rejoice in the houses which are compatible with their natures and where they may express their natures comfortably. Planets have houses in which they rejoice (such as Venus in the 5th), and also signs (such as Venus in Taurus).

Local Determination: How a planet's general nature is specified to a particular area of life due to the house it is in. This phrase is a technical term in the work of Morin.

Lots: A position derived from the position of three other parts of a chart. Normally, the distance between two places is measured in zodiacal order from one to the other, and this distance is projected forward from some other place (usually the Ascendant): where the counting stops, is the Lot.

Luminaries: The Sun and the Moon.

Lunar Nodes: The points where the Moon intersects the plane of the ecliptic. The *South Node* is where the Moon crosses it into southern latitude, and the *North Node* where she crossed into northern latitude. Traditionally the *North Node* is considered to be equivalent to a benefic, whereas the *South Node* is equivalent to a malefic.

Malefics: A planet which requires a great effort to be productive, which brings trouble and restrictions. They are unproductive and prone to extremism. Planets malefic by nature are Saturn and

Mars. The waning Moon and in some cases Mercury may also be considered as malefics.

Masculine Planets: Sun, Saturn, Jupiter, Mars, and sometimes Mercury.

MC (Medium Coeli), Midheaven: Where the zodiac crosses the southern meridian, and in quadrant houses the cusp of the 10th house.

Minor Dignity: A dignity apart from the usual five essential dignities (for example, **hayz**).

Moiety: One-half of an **orb**, i.e. the number of degrees on either side of a planet or other point, which defines its special range of influence.

Mundane Astrology: The branch of astrology concerned with predictions for political, social, financial, religious, or military events.

Mutual Interaction: see **Mutual Reception**.

Mutual Reception: When two planets are placed in each other's domiciles, they are in mutual reception: they "host" each other. Bonatti suggested that these two planets should aspect each other for a mutual reception. On the other hand, Abū Ma'shar, Ibn Ezra and William Lilly suggested if these two planets are in each other's dignities by domicile, exaltation, or other rulerships, they do not need an aspect to create a mutual interaction: this is called "generosity."

Natal Astrology: The branch of astrology which casts a chart for someone's birth, with techniques for determining the native's personal potentials, tendencies, motivations, accidents that he may experience, financial situation, relationships, and so on.

Nocturnal Planets: Moon, Venus, and Mars.

North Node: See **Lunar Nodes**.

Ninth-parts: A subdivision of each sign into nine parts, each formed of 3° 20'.

Novenaria: See **Ninth-parts**.

Occidental: See **Western**.

Orb. A span of degrees on either side of a body or point, which indicates a range of power. See also **moiety**.

Oriental: See **Eastern**.

Paran: Star or star groups that fall upon angles at the same time that another significant constellation or planet is also upon the angles. They are viewed as attendants. In ancient astrology the term was also applied to the constellations that ascended with the zodiacal decans.

Peregrine: See **Alien**.

Perihelion: The point in the orbit of a planet where it is nearest to the Sun.

Powerful Planet: Refers to a planet's capacity to fulfill the things it represents naturally or accidentally. A powerful planet may have an impact on an end result. The power of a planet is determined through its position in the chart, including its essential and accidental placement and some other factors.

Primary Directions: A method of directions based on primary motion or the diurnal rotation of the heavens.

Quadruplicity: A qualitative division of the signs into three groups, each with four signs. These three groups are called cardinal, fixed and mutable signs. Aries, Cancer, Libra, and Capricorn are cardinal signs; Taurus, Leo, Scorpio, and Aquarius are fixed signs; Gemini, Virgo, Sagittarius, and Pisces are mutable signs.

Reception: When a planet host another planet in the sign which it rules. When two planets are in **mutual reception**, both of them gain power and they act as if they are in their own rulerships.

Releaser: A planet or point directed by **primary directions**, to predict the length of life and other life crises.

Retrograde: When a planet seems to slow down, stop, and turn backwards in the zodiac. It is one of the most important debilities. A retrograde significator is passive and has difficulty in fulfilling its promises.

SAN: See **Syzygy.**

Sect: A division of charts, planets, and signs into "diurnal/day" and "nocturnal/night." Charts are diurnal if the Sun is above the horizon, otherwise they are nocturnal.

Solar Arcs: A predictive technique in which each planet is directed at the same rate in which the Sun is directed in secondary progressions, with 1 year = 1 degree. There is no retrograde motion in this technique because it does not represent the native's psychology (as in progressions).

South Node: See **Lunar Nodes**.

Succeedent Houses: Houses which follows the angular houses: the 2nd, 5th, 8th, and 11th.

Syzygy: The pre-natal New or Full Moon degree. The syzygy before birth is used in many natal techniques, such as in predicting longevity or determining the **victor of the chart**.

Terms: A division of each sign into five parts; each term is ruled by a single planet. For example, Venus is the term ruler of Cancer between 7° – 13°. The luminaries do not rule any terms in the three standard sets of terms (which are the Egyptian, Chaldean, and Ptolemaic).

Tolerance: See **Orb.**

Triplicity Lords: A group of three planets ruling over each set of signs in a **triplicity**, divided into the day, night, and partnering rulers. Triplicity lords were used extensively by Dorotheus and later astrologers, to understand the support given to a particular point in the chart.

Triplicity: A classification of the signs into groups of three, by their elements: Fire, Earth, Air and Water signs. Aries, Leo, and Sagittarius are Fire signs; Taurus, Virgo, and Capricorn are Earth signs; Gemini, Libra, and Aquarius are Air signs; Cancer, Scorpio, and Pisces are Water signs.

Twelfth-parts: A division of each sign into twelve parts, each formed of 2° 30'.

Via Combusta ("Burned path"): The area between 15° Libra and 15° Scorpio. Considered to be a debilitating area, especially for the Moon. According to some astrologers like Māshā'allāh and al-Bīrūnī, it is between 19° Libra and 3° Scorpio, which are the degrees of the fall of the luminaries.

Victor: The planet which gets the highest score over one or more positions, according to the table of dignities; the most dignified planet of any specific zodiacal degree.

Victor of the chart: It is the key of the whole chart; the key for the native's life. It represents the force that dominates the native's life. It may also be considered as describing the primary characteristics of the native.

Void of Course: When a planet, especially the Moon, remains out of orb of any aspect (or does not complete an exact aspect) so long as it is in its current sign.

Weak Planet: A planet which has difficulties in fulfilling its natural and accidental promises, and cannot bring a result or cannot impact the final result. Weakness is determined through a planet's essential and accidental placement, along with other factors.

Well disposed: When the lord of the sign in which some planet is located, is in a good **zodiacal state**.

Western: Planets which set after the Sun. Planets which are western of the Sun have difficulty in fulfilling their promises. They have anti-social methods which may be questioned.

Western Quarters: The quarters of the chart between the MC-DSC and IC-ASC.

Whole Signs: The oldest system of assigning house topics. In this system, each sign is a house, so there are no intercepted signs. It was used by many astrologers, sometimes along with quadrant systems (such as Alchabitius semi-arcs, Placidus, etc.).

Zodiac: The belt of twelve signs.

Zodiacal State: A planet's strength (dignity) or weakness, especially in terms of the type of house, sign (dignity), and relationship to its lord.

References

Abū Bakr, *On Nativities*, trans. and ed. Benjamin N. Dykes, in Dykes 2010 (*Persian Nativities* II).

Al-Bīrūnī, Muhammad b. Ahmad, *The Book of Instruction in the Elements of the Art of Astrology*, trans. R. Ramsay Wright (London: Luzac & Co., 1934)

Al-Khayyāt, Abū 'Ali, *The Judgments of Nativities*, trans. and ed. Benjamin N. Dykes, in Dykes 2009.

Al-Qabīsī, *The Introduction to Astrology*, eds. Charles Burnett, Keiji Yamamoto, Michio Yano (London and Turin: The Warburg Institute, 2004)

Al-Tabarī, 'Umar, *Three Books on Nativities*, trans. and ed. Benjamin N. Dykes, in Dykes 2010.

Bills, Rex E., *The Rulership Book: A Directory of Astrological Correspondences* (Richmond, VA: Macoy Publishing & Masonic Supply Co., Inc., 1971)

Bonatti, Guido, *The Book of Astronomy*, trans. and ed. Benjamin N. Dykes (Golden Valley, MN: The Cazimi Press, 2007)

Dykes, Benjamin, trans. and ed., *Persian Nativities I: Māshā'allāh & Abū 'Ali* (Minneapolis, MN: The Cazimi Press, 2009)

Dykes, Benjamin, trans. and ed., *Persian Nativities II: 'Umar al-Tabarī & Abū Bakr* (Minneapolis, MN: The Cazimi Press, 2010)

Dykes, Benjamin trans. and ed., *Introductions to Traditional Astrology: Abū Ma'shar & al-Qabīsī* (Minneapolis, MN: The Cazimi Press, 2010)

Firmicus Maternus, *Mathesis*, trans. and ed. Benjamin N. Dykes (Minneapolis, MN: The Cazimi Press, forthcoming)

Hall, Judy, *The Astrology Bible: The Definitive Guide to the Zodiac* (New York, NY: Sterling Publishing Co., Inc., 2005)

Lilly, William, *Christian Astrology*, ed. David R. Roell (Abingdon, MD: Astrology Center of America, 2004)

Morin, Jean-Baptiste, *The Morinus System of Horoscope Interpretation* (*Astrologia Gallica* Book 21), trans. Richard S. Baldwin (Washington, DC: The American Federation of Astrologers, Inc., 1974)

Parker, Julia and Derek, *Parker's Astrology: The Definitive Guide to Using Astrology in Every Aspect of Your Life* (New York, NY: DK Publishing, Inc., 2001)

Ptolemy, Claudius, *Tetrabiblos*, trans. F.E. Robbins (Cambridge and London: Harvard University Press, 1940)

Schoener, Johannes, *On the Judgments of Nativities*, trans. and ed. Benjamin N. Dykes (Minneapolis, MN: The Cazimi Press, forthcoming)

Zoller, Robert, *Diploma Course in Medieval Astrology* (Robert Zoller and New Library, Ltd., 2002)

Zoller, Robert, *Medieval Astrology Foundation Course* (Robert Zoller and New Library, Ltd., 2000)

About the AstroArt Astrology School

Since its establishment in 2005, the AstroArt Astrology School aims at bringing sound and qualified astrological knowledge to society. In the constant pursuit of this goal over the past 13 years, it has succeeded in distinguishing itself and has been a pioneer in many areas, providing high standards of astrological education and creating a lively astrological community in Turkey.

The popularity of AstroArt derives mainly from our ability to offer a graded educational curriculum, covering both traditional and modern astrological techniques. We also offer many different specialty classes for those wishing to improve their knowledge after completing the certificate course. Our specialty courses cover a wide range of topics, namely: medical astrology, financial astrology, mundane astrology, esoteric astrology, Uranian astrology, cosmic astrology, horary astrology, and electional astrology. These classes are run by 11 different tutors who are expert in their chosen subjects.

We have also widened our teaching group with international lecturers, including Glenn Perry on astro-psychology and Aleksandar Imsiragic on Hermetic astrology. Gaye Döşer also presents on cosmic astrology and healing. We have also expanded our esoteric astrology studies by applying Islamic mysticism (Sufism) to astrology.

We are proud to have created many ways of providing knowledge on a country-wide basis: our online interactive classes and our web broadcasts through Astrology TV derive from this mission. So far we reach Germany, Holland, and Cyprus, as well as many other cities, by which we have brought a solid education to those who are physically unable to attend the school.

Our school also has been a pioneer in bringing its educational program into an internationally recognized Turkish university (Girne American University), and hence providing recognition with a certificate of acknowledgment for astrology education at the university level. Certificates are given and signed by the rectorate, and classes are held on university premises. This program started in 2014 and students should exhibit 75% eligibility in obtaining the certificate.

Apart from online web broadcasting, we have established our own publishing company to provide our own textbooks, and we have also liaised with international astrologers who provide their knowledge for Turkish readers, including Glenn Perry, Lea Imsiragic, Deborah Houlding, and Benjamin Dykes.

Our school is situated in Istanbul, which has been a bridge between Eastern and Western cultures for centuries. Hence, apart from teaching and distributing knowledge we have the vision to create an internationally recognized social environment for followers of astrology, sharing astrological developments on a worldwide scale. To that end, since 2012 we have organized the annual "International Astrology Days" in March at the spring equinox. Every year we provide a special discussion topic for our international guest speakers to elaborate on for the benefit of the public, in addition to seminars and workshops for astrology students. We publish the outcome as a separate volume.

International Astrology Days Activities in Istanbul (since 2012)

Our school is now a proud affiliate of ISAR (International Society for Astrological Research), through which it is now able to provide its students the opportunity to obtain an internationally recognized proficiency certificate for their astrology education. We believe that this is a great chance for students who want to enjoy a worldwide mutual understanding for their level of astrological knowledge, as well as being a member of a school whose name is amongst the top names of worldwide schools.

An ISAR-affiliated school offers advantages for expanding one's borders and liaise within a worldwide network which is constantly in tune with the current developments of astrological knowledge, as one of the prime purposes of the ISAR Affiliated School Program is to create an educational resource for astrologers worldwide. ISAR only recognizes those schools of astrology whose curriculum enables its students of astrology to acquire mutually accepted global standards of knowledge, contributing to a worldwide professional education.

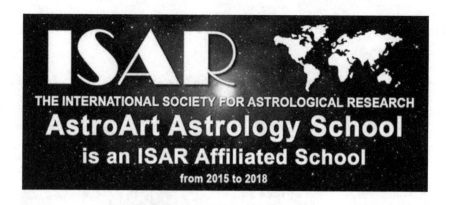

Students who wish to obtain an ISAR CAP (Certificate of Astrological Proficiency) certificate first should first complete our school's educational program and pass the exams with at least 70%, and then apply to ISAR CAP. ISAR requires proof of proficiency in three areas:

- ISAR Ethics training
- ISAR Consulting Skill training
- ISAR Competency Exam

Applicants who successfully complete those steps receive their ISAR CAP certificate, which is currently the highest certification in the world of astrology. Detailed further information can be obtained from the school's administration or from the link given below:

www.astrolojiokulu.com

We would hereby like to take the liberty to indicate our pleasure at being part of such a distinguished society, and emphasize our gratitude for those who helped us on that road. We also thank the community of ISAR directors for welcoming us, with special thanks to Alex Imsiragic who suggested and initiated the idea in the first place.

On Behalf of the AstroArt Astrology School Istanbul,
Öner Döşer, AMA, ISAR CAP
Director

Books Published in English by

ASTROART ASTROLOGY SCHOOL

Financial Significators
Öner Döşer

Marriage Significators
Öner Döşer

Professional Significators
Öner Döşer

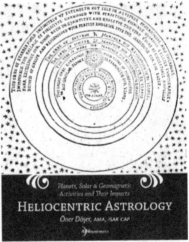

Heliocentric Astrology
Öner Döşer

Books Published in English by

ASTROART ASTROLOGY SCHOOL

The Art of Horary Astrology
Öner Döşer

**Karma, Fate, Free Will
and Astrology**
Öner Döşer

**An Islamic View of
Hermetic Knowledge**
Öner Döşer

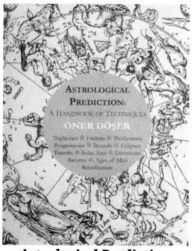

Astrological Prediction
Öner Döşer